AF600507

A STUDY OF THE JURIDIC STATUS OF LAYMEN IN THE WRITING OF THE MEDIEVAL CANONISTS

The writing of this dissertation was conducted under the direction of Dr. Stephan Kuttner, J.U.D., S.J.D., J.C.D., as major professor, and was approved by Rev. Frederick R. McManus, A.B., J.C.D., and Rev. John J. McGrath, A.B., LL.B., J.C.D., as readers.

THE CATHOLIC UNIVERSITY OF AMERICA
CANON LAW STUDIES
No. 395

A Study of the Juridic Status of Laymen in the Writing of the Medieval Canonists

A DISSERTATION

SUBMITTED TO THE FACULTY OF THE SCHOOL OF CANON LAW OF THE CATHOLIC UNIVERSITY OF AMERICA IN PARTIAL FULFILLMENT OF THE REQUIREMENTS FOR THE DEGREE OF DOCTOR OF CANON LAW

BY

REV. RONALD J. COX, S.T.L., J.C.L.
PRIEST OF THE DIOCESE OF STEUBENVILLE

THE CATHOLIC UNIVERSITY OF AMERICA PRESS
WASHINGTON, D.C.
1959

NIHIL OBSTAT:
JOHN J. MCGRATH, A.B., LL.B., J.C.D.
Censor Deputatus

IMPRIMATUR:
✠ JOHN KING MUSSIO, D.D., J.C.D.
Episcopus Steubenvicensis

September 8, 1958

Printed by The Abbey Press, St. Meinrad, Indiana, U.S.A.

DEDICATED
TO MY
BELOVED PARENTS

FOREWORD

In recent years there has been a great revival of scholastic interest in the history of the development of Canon Law. Of special importance as objects of research have been the writings of the large body of canonists who lived from the twelfth through the fourteenth centuries. Studies in increasing number are being undertaken to determine what part these commentators on the Church's discipline have played in the shaping of many of our modern institutions, both ecclesiastical and civil. An immense project is already well underway to make available to scholars printed editions of the many canonistic works which up to this time have been extant only in manuscript form, scattered throughout the libraries of Europe. As a result of this activity and research it has become apparent to historians and canonists alike that the medieval canonists have a much more important place in the history of ideas than has heretofore been imagined.

This dissertation has for its objective a study of the teaching of the medieval canonists regarding the juridic status of the layman in the Church, particularly in relation to the exercise of the Church's power of jurisdiction. It comprises a series of essays presenting the results of the writer's research into several areas of Church authority and administration. As such, it cannot pretend to give a complete picture of the place of the layman, as the canonists saw him, in the life of the medieval Church.

Purposely excluded from this study is any specific treatment of the doctrine of the canonists on the relations between Church and State, although this certainly involves the question of laymen and Church authority. Also, the complicated institute of clerical immunity from the jurisdiction of secular tribunals will not be a direct object of study. Throughout, the emphasis will be upon the status of laymen considered precisely as laymen, that is, as distinct from the clergy, rather than as members of the *corpus mysticum* or as part of the *fidelium universitas*.

The sources of this study are of necessity limited to the printed works available to the writer, though several unedited commentaries will be cited from time to time through secondary source material. While the number of canonistic writings examined is not large, the writer believes it sufficient to provide a cross section of canonical thought on the topics treated.

The writer wishes to express his sincere gratitude to the Most Reverend John King Mussio, D.D., J.C.D., Bishop of Steubenville, for the opportunity to undertake graduate studies in Canon Law; to Professor Stephan Kuttner, J.U.D., S.J.D., J.C.D., for his scholarly guidance and many kindnesses; and to the other members of the Faculty of the School of the Canon Law at the Catholic University of America for their profitable instruction and kind assistance.

TABLE OF CONTENTS

CHAPTER ONE

PRENOTES

The period extending from the *Decretum* of Gratian (1140) to Joannes Andreae (d. 1348) is generally recognized as the age of the classical canonists.[1] Centralization of administration in the Church during these years, and a large increase in the amount of legislation enacted by the Holy See, brought about a great need for specialists in ecclesiastical jurisprudence. This need was met, under the patronage of the Church, by the universities which sprang up throughout Europe, particularly from the twelfth century onward. They produced a great number of trained lawyers and judges, and gave to the Church an impressive line of lawyer Popes, beginning with Alexander III (1159-1181).

The writings of the canonists who lived in this golden age are to be the principal objects of investigation in this study. The years after Joannes Andreae saw a decline in constructive effort in canonical science. Important canonists wrote during the fourteenth and fifteenth centuries, to be sure; but the canonistic works of this period are all too often filled with repetitions, summaries, and quotations of the great legists who wrote before them.[2] However, since such slavish conformity is but a reflection of the great influence of the classical canonists, passages from the writings of several of these later jurists will be cited in this study.

The first article of this preliminary chapter is divided into two parts. Section 1 is presented as historical back-

[1] Stickler, Review of *Medieval Papalism*, by W. Ullmann, "Concerning the Political Theories of the Medieval Canonists," *Traditio*, VII (1949-1951), 453.

[2] Van Hove, *Prolegomena ad Codicem Juris Canonici* (2. ed., Mechliniae: H. Dessain, 1945), p. 472 (hereafter cited *Prolegomena*).

ground, and contains a very short summary of the more significant events in the development of the science of Canon Law in the twelfth and thirteenth centuries. Emphasis is placed upon the history of the formation of the *Corpus Juris Canonici.* The second part of the article is chiefly biographical. It lists the individual canonists whose writings have been investigated in the preparation of this dissertation, with a few words about the activity of each as a canonist, and information as to the printed editions of their works the writer has consulted.

ARTICLE I. THE CANONICAL PERIOD TO BE STUDIED

SECTION 1. THE DEVELOPMENT OF THE SCIENCE OF CANON LAW FROM GRATIAN TO JOANNES ANDREAE

The twelfth century saw the growth of the Canon Law into a strict juridic science.[3] Its development coincided with the revival of the study of Roman jurisprudence, particularly in the highly commercial Lombard cities. This intellectual activity was responsible for the rapid rise of the University of Bologna as a center for the study of Roman Law. The fame of this school was enhanced very early by the teaching and work of two men. One of them, Irnerius (d. after 1125), was influential in the introduction of systematic study of the entire *Corpus Juris Civilis*

[3] This historical summary is taken for the most part from information in Van Hove, *Prolegomena,* pp. 337-382, 423-527; Stickler *Historia juris canonici latini, I, Historia fontium* (Augustae Taurinorum, 1950), pp. 197-276 (hereafter cited *Historia*). For the effect of this legal development on medieval Church institutes and extensive bibliography see Feine, *Kirchliche Rechtsgeschichte,* I, *Die katholische Kirche* (Weimar: Hermann Nachfolger, 1955). Brief outlines of the growth of the science of Canon Law are given in Tierney, *Foundations of the Conciliar Theory, The Contribution of the Medieval Canonists from Gratian to the Great Schism,* Cambridge Studies in Medieval Life and Thought, N.S., vol. 4 (Cambridge: Cambridge University Press, 1955), pp. 14-18 (hereafter cited *Conciliar Theory*); Le Bras, "Canon Law," *The Legacy of the Middle Ages* (eds. C. Crump and E. Jacob, Oxford: Clarendon Press, 1951), pp. 321-361.

as a part of the ordinary legal education. The other important figure was Gratian, the Father of the science of Canon Law.[4]

The appearance, about the year 1140, of Gratian's *Concordia discordantium canonum,* later known as the *Decreta* or *Decretum,* marks the great turning point in the history of medieval Canon Law.[5] As a synthesis of earlier collections of canons having as their sources the Scriptures, the Fathers, the canons of Councils, papal decretals, and civil laws, it brought to a close several centuries of painstaking assembly of the authorities of the past.[6] The *Decretum* was, however, much more than a compilation. It was an instructive textbook, which applied the new scholastic and juridic principles of criticism to hundreds of systematically arranged texts in order to bring into harmony their many divergencies and contradictions. It is Gratian's glory that he turned the many heterogeneous canons into the funda-

[4] Sokolich, *Canonical Provisions for Universities and Colleges,* The Catholic University of America Canon Law Studies, n. 373 (Washington, D.C.: The Catholic University of America Press, 1956), pp. 7-8; Kuttner, "The Father of the Science of Canon Law," *The Jurist,* I (1941), 12-14.

[5] The work was certainly compiled before 1142. Of Gratian's early life, little is known. He was a Camaldolese monk of the monastery of Saints Felix and Nabor in Bologna, where he taught theology, and probably died before 1160.—Stickler, *Historia,* p. 204.

[6] Kuttner, "The Scientific Investigation of Medieval Canon Law: The Need and the Opportunity," *Speculum,* XXIV (1949), p. 495. The Decretum made obsolete the famous collections of Burchard, Anselm of Lucca, and Ivo of Chartres. For the collections prior to Gratian, see P. Fournier et G. Le Bras, *Histoire des collections canoniques en occident* (2 vols., Paris, 1931-1932), esp. vol. 2; Stickler, *Historia,* pp. 142-195; Van Hove, *Prolegomena,* pp. 312-337. The state of canonical source material at the time Gratian undertook to write his *Concordia* has been described as a "confused mass of ancient and recent, general and particular, ecclesiastical and secular, authentic and forged, disciplinary and doctrinal texts, taken by the collectors from oecumenical and particular statutes and patristic writings, from penitentials, formularies, liturgical books and Sacred Scripture."—Kuttner, "The Father of the Science of Canon Law," p. 4.

mental text of a new universal science, a well organized system of ecclesiastical law.[7]

Although it was only a private work, the *Decretum* was universally accepted by the schools as the basic text for the study of the new science. Gratian had classified the more important texts, and had almost succeeded in separating ecclesiastical law from the rapidly developing scientific theology. Yet many inconsistencies in the text of the *Decretum* remained to be explored; new legislation and new problems facing the universal Church left the disciples of Gratian with plenty of material for speculation.[8]

The first canonists met this challenge. Quite naturally they employed for their work the same scholastic methods used by the students of the Roman Law at Bologna. A large production of marginal notation (*glossae*) on the *Decretum* soon appeared, much of it later being incorporated into more systematic treatises known as *Summae* and *Quaestiones*. From Bologna study of the science spread to other Universities throughout Europe. The first fifty years after Gratian saw a number of influential *Summae* produced by the Decretists, as the commentators on the *Decretum* are now known. To this period belong the *Summae* of PAUCAPALEA (ca. 1148), RUFINUS (ca. 1157-1159), SIMON OF BISIGNANO (ca. 1177-1179), SICARD OF CREMONA (ca. 1179-1181), and, most important of all, HUGUCCIO (ca. 1190).[9]

From the middle of the twelfth century the history of the science of Canon Law was affected by still another development. About this time the Roman Pontiffs began to issue, in ever increasing numbers, authoritative solutions in the form of responses to questions proposed about judicial cases and matters of discipline. Practical recognition of the Pope as supreme lawmaker in the Church, and as the interpreter of his law, a growing centralization of ad-

[7] Cf. Kuttner, "The Father of the Science of Canon Law," pp. 6-7, 15.

[8] Le Bras, "Canon Law," p. 326.

[9] Van Hove, *Prolegomena*, pp. 423-442. Unfortunately, the great work of Huguccio is unedited.

ministration within the Church, the more scientific state of the law itself—all were factors contributing to this growth in the number of papal decretals. But what is more important, the Chair of Peter was frequently occupied by skilled canonists.[10]

The canonists soon turned their attention to the new body of decretals. They recognized that these papal responses, meant for particular cases, could well serve as general norms of law. They began early to make collections of these *extravagantes* (*decretales extra decreta vagantes*). Small at first, the compilations grew in size and value, especially after the canons of the III Lateran Council (1179) were incorporated into them. About the year 1190, one of these collections was made the subject of lectures at the Universities along with the *Decretum.* This innovation brought a temporary halt to the production of *Summae* on Gratian's work, as the canonists busied themselves making glosses and *Summae* on the new compilation.[11]

The collection responsible for this change of emphasis was the *Breviarium extravagantium* of Bernard of Pavia (d. 1213), compiled between 1188 and 1192. Of special importance in that its arrangement of five books subdivided into titles became the standard form of all later decretal collections, this work became known as the *Compilatio Prima.* It was the first of a series of five of the more important collections accepted and commented upon by the Universities, the so-called *Quinque compilationes antiquae.* Two of these collections were promulgated to the school at Bologna as binding, universal law—the *Compilatio Tertia* (1210), a collection of Pope Innocent III, and the *Compilatio Quinta* (1226), issued by Pope Honorius III.[12]

[10] Van Hove, *Prolegomena,* pp. 349-350 for the substance of this paragraph.

[11] Kuttner, "Bernardus Compostellanus Antiquus," *Traditio* I (1943), 283-285; Van Hove, *Prolegomena,* p. 349.

[12] Stickler, *Historia,* pp. 225-236; Kuttner, "Bernardus Compostellanus Antiquus," p. 285.—The *Compilationes* are edited by Friedberg, *Quinque compilationes antiquae nec non collectio canonum Lipsiensis*

In the period after Huguccio a number of commentaries were written on the decretal collections, among them the *Summa* of Bernard of Pavia on his own compilation. Shortly after the turn of the century the attention of the schools again was turned to the *Decretum,* in an attempt to interpret and explain its canons in the light of the more recent legislation. This attention resulted in a new form of canonical writing, the *Apparatus glossarum,* in which the author added his own comments to a well ordered collection of the works of other glossators. The *Apparatus* of LAURENTIUS HISPANUS (ca. 1210-1215), the *Glossa Palatina* (ca. 1210-1215), and the *Apparatus* of JOANNES TEUTONICUS (ca. 1215- 1217), received as the *Glossa ordinaria* by the schools, are among the more important of these works.[13]

In September of 1234, Pope Gregory IX gave great impetus to the new science by sending to the Universities at Bologna and Paris a comprehensive official collection, containing for the most part decretals found in the *Quinque compilationes antiquae,* along with 195 *capitula* from his own decrees. The compilation was made by St. Raymond of Peñafort, who eliminated many contradictions and a great deal of unnecessary detail from the various *responsa* included in the collection. The Decretals were to have official force everywhere, superseding all earlier compilations, and were to be considered as having been promulgated as of 1234. The work was usually referred to as the *Liber Extravagantium,* the *Liber Extra,* or simply *X.*[14]

A host of important canonists wrote between the promulgation of Gregory's Decretals and the end of the century. POPE INNOCENT IV (Sinibaldus Fliscus, d. 1254) and HENRI-

(Gras, 1956 [first published at Leipzig, 1882]). The *Compilatio Secunda* appeared after the collection of Innocent, and contained material from earlier collections. The *Compilatio Quarta* included canons of the IV Lateran Council (1215) and other decretals of Innocent.

[13] Kuttner, "Bernardus Compostellanus Antiquus," pp. 288-289; cf. Van Hove, *Prolegomena,* pp. 429-432, 443-453.

[14] Stickler, *Historia,* pp. 242-251; Van Hove, *Prolegomena,* pp. 358-360.

CUS DE SEGUSIO, better known as HOSTIENSIS (d. 1271), are the most prominent. Among the other canonists who greatly influenced the jurisprudence of their time should be mentioned VINCENTIUS HISPANUS (d. 1245), BERNARD OF PARMA (d. 1266), whose commentary on the Decretals was received as the *Glossa ordinaria,* RAYMOND OF PENAFORT (d. 1275), GOFFREDUS DE TRANO (d. 1245), ABBAS ANTIQUUS (d. 1296), GUILIELMUS DURANTIS (d. 1296), and GUIDO DE BAYSIO (d. 1313).[15]

The issuance of papal decretals did not end with the Decretals of Gregory. Popes Innocent IV (1234-1254), Gregory X (1271-1276) and Nicholas III (1277-1280) all promulgated official collections of their responses and legislation. When Boniface VIII began his reign in 1294, there was need for another collection to reorganize these *Novellae,* as they were called, and bring them up to date. To do this, Boniface promulgated as universal law on March 3, 1298, the *Liber Sextus Decretalium,* which cancelled the juridic effect of all post-Gregorian decretals to which it did not make reference.[16]

The historical period to be investigated in this study ends with the promulgation of the *Liber Sextus,* and the composition of its *Glossa ordinaria,* written before 1303 by JOANNES ANDREAE (d. 1348). However the body of canons now known as the *Corpus Juris Canonici* was not completed until some years later. Included in the *Corpus* are, in addition to the *Decretum Gratiani* and the official collections of Gregory IX and Boniface VIII, the *Clementinae,* transmitted to the universities by Pope John XXII in 1317, and the *Collectio viginti extravagantium Joannis XXII* and the *Extravagantes communes,* both private collections of decretals compiled after the reign of Pope John XXII (1316-1334).[17]

[15] Van Hove, *Prolegomena,* pp. 473 ff.

[16] Stickler, *Historia,* pp. 251-264.

[17] Stickler, *Historia,* pp. 264-276.

SECTION 2. THE CANONISTS

The number of canonists who wrote during the centuries after the appearance of the *Decretum* of Gratian is very large. Even more impressive is the voluminousness of their writings. Unfortunately, many works of the Decretists and Decretalists remain unedited, and of the printed editions, many must be classified as rare books, for the most part sixteenth century editions. The following biographical listing of the canonists whose works are used in this study is presented for the convenience of the reader.[18]

A. Canonists who wrote between Gratian and the Decretals of Gregory IX

PAUCAPALEA: A pupil of Gratian, Paucapalea is known as the first of the Decretists. He was responsible for a number of additions to the *Decretum* which were later incorporated into the manuscripts and known as *Paleae*. His *Summa* was written sometime between 1140 and 1148.[19]

ROLANDUS BANDINELLI (Pope Alexander III): Also a pupil of Gratian, Rolandus became the first of the great canonist Popes in 1159. Though hampered in his reform efforts by a nineteen-year struggle with the emperor Frederick I, Alexander issued many papal decretals, a number of which were incorporated in the official collection of Gregory IX, and managed to summon the III Lateran Council (1179) before his death in 1181. His *Summa* was written before he became Pope, sometime before 1148.[20]

[18] First references in the footnotes of this section refer to the writer's source of biographical information; the second to the printed editions consulted. All quotations from the *Decretum* of Gratian, the Decretals of Gregory IX, and the *Liber Sextus* of Boniface VIII are taken from the *Corpus Juris Canonici* (ed. Lipsiensis secunda, post Aemilii Richteri curas... instruxit Aemilius Friedberg, 2 vols., Lipsiae, 1879-1881).

[19] Van Hove, *Prolegomena*, pp. 433-434; Tierney, *Conciliar Theory*, p. 261.—*Die Summa des Paucapalea über das Decretum Gratiani* (J. F. v. Schulte, ed., Giessen, 1890 [hereafter cited Paucapalea]).

[20] Van Hove, *Prolegomena*, p. 432; Tierney, *Conciliar Theory*, p.

RUFINUS: Rufinus was the author of the most important *Summa* on the *Decretum* to appear before that of Huguccio (1188-1190). It was composed between 1157 and 1159. Little is known of Rufinus other than that he taught at Bologna, and subsequently became bishop of Assisi and archbishop of Sorrento (1180). He also preached at the opening of the III Lateran Council in 1179.[21]

SUMMA PARISIENSIS: The work of an unknown author, the *Summa Parisiensis* is of great value for the information which it has left us regarding the *Decretum* of Gratian, and because of its early date. It was recently edited for the first time by T. P. McLaughlin, who believes it to have been produced at Paris as early as 1160.[22]

STEPHEN OF TOURNAI: A native of Orleans, Stephen studied both at Paris and at Bologna, and later became bishop of Tournai. His *Summa* dates from the 1160's.[23]

SIMON OF BISIGNANO: A member of the school at Bologna. His *Summa* on the *Decretum* appeared between 1177 and 1179.[24]

HUGUCCIO: A native of Pisa and a teacher at Bologna, Huguccio was the most famous of the twelfth century De-

262; cf. Hughes, *A History of the Church* (3 vols., New York: Sheed and Ward, 1947-1949), II, 303-313.—*Die Summa Magistri Rolandi nachmals Papstes Alexander III* (ed., F. Thaner, Innsbruck, 1874 [hereafter cited Rolandus, *Summa*]).

[21] Van Hove, *Prolegomena*, p. 434; Tierney, *Conciliar Theory*, p. 262; Kuttner, "Bernardus Compostellanus Antiquus," p. 280, note. —*Die Summa Decretorum des Magister Rufinus* (ed. H. Singer, Paderborn, 1902 [hereafter cited Rufinus, *Summa*]).

[22] The *Summa Parisiensis on the Decretum Gratiani* (ed. T. P. McLaughlin, Toronto, 1952), pp. xvii, xix-xx, xxxii (hereafter cited *Summa Paris.*).

[23] Van Hove, *Prolegomena*, p . 434; Tierney, *Conciliar Theory*, p. 262.—*Die Summa des Stephanus Tornacensis über* das *Decretum Gratiani* (ed. J. F. v. Schulte, Giessen, 1891, [hereafter cited Stephanus *Summa*]).

[24] Van Hove, *Prolegomena*, p. 435. The *Summa* is unedited.

cretists. His massive *Summa* was written between 1188 and 1190. In 1190 he became bishop of Ferrara.[25]

BERNARDUS PAPIENSIS: The compiler of the *Compilatio Prima,* Bernardus wrote a number of canonical works, including an important *Summa decretalium* on his own compilation, a *Summa de matrimonio,* and a *Summa de electione.* He died in 1214.[26]

JOANNES TEUTONICUS: Professor at the University of Bologna, Joannes Teutonicus is remembered most as the author of an extensive gloss on the *Decretum.* Written between the IV Lateran Council (1215) and 1217, it was soon accepted by the schools as the *Glossa ordinaria* on Gratian's work. Joannes also wrote glosses on the Decretal collections, including an important gloss on the *Compilatio Quarta,* of which he was probably the compiler. He died in 1245 or 1246.[27]

ST. RAYMOND OF PENAFORT: A native of Spain, Raymond studied and taught at Bologna. He entered the Dominican Order, and became chaplain, penitentiary, and legal counselor to Pope Gregory IX. While his fame as a canonist rests largely on his work as compiler of the official Decretals of this Pope, Raymond was the author of several canonical treatises. The most influential of these, his *Summa de*

[25] Van Hove, *Prolegomena,* pp. 435-436. The *Summa* is unedited.

[26] Van Hove, *Prolegomena,* pp. 356, 447-448, 450.—*Summa decretalium Bernardi Papiensis* (ed. E. Laspeyres [1860], Graz: Akademische Druck-U. Verlagsanstalt, 1956). The *Summa de matrimonio* and the *Summa de electione* are included as appendices in this edition.

[27] Van Hove, *Prolegomena,* p. 431; Stickler, *Historia,* p. 235.—*Glossa ordinaria* to the *Decretum,* in *Decretum Gratiani emendatum... cum glossis* (2 vols., Romae, 1592). The *Glossa ordinaria* in the printed editions of the *Decretum* is the revised version of Joannes' gloss, written by Bartholomaeus of Brescia (between 1240 and 1246), who adapted the work to the intervening decretal legislation. Cf. Kuttner, "Bernardus Compostellanus Antiquus," p. 289; Van Hove, *op. cit.,* pp. 431-432. The gloss on the *Compilatio Quarta* is found as an addendum to the *Compilatio* in *Antiquae collectiones decretalium* (ed. A. Augustinus, Ilerdae, 1576).

poenitentia, is cited in this study. It was written between 1222 and 1225, and revised betwen 1234 and 1236. Raymond died in 1275.[28]

B. Canonists who wrote between the Decretals of Gregory IX and Joannes Andreae

BERNARD OF PARMA: Born at Parma in the beginning of the thirteenth century, Bernard was a pupil of the famous glossators Tancred and Vincentius Hispanus. Using materials from their writings and from the *Apparatus* of Laurentius Hispanus, he wrote the *glossa* on the Decretals of Gregory IX which came to be accepted as the *Glossa ordinaria* by the schools. At least four versions of this gloss were prepared. The first dates from 1241; the last between 1263 and 1266, the probable year of Bernard's death.[29]

INNOCENT IV (Sinibaldus Fliscus): A native of Genoa, Sinibaldus became Pope Innocent IV in 1243. Prior to that time he taught at Bologna, and was bishop of Albenga (1235). One of the greatest of the medieval jurists, Innocent wrote his important commentary on the Decretals of Gregory IX about the year 1251. In 1245, 1246, and 1253, he added to the official decretal collection. He died in 1254.[30]

[28] Stickler, *Historia,* p. 241; Van Hove, *Prolegomena,* pp. 358, 513. The dates are those given by Kuttner, "Zur Entstehungsgeschichte der Summa de casibus des hl. Raymund von Penyafort," *Zeitschrift der Savigny Stiftung fur Rechtsgeschichte, Kanonistische Abteilung,* XXXIX (1953), pp. 434-435.—*Summa Sti. Raymundi de Peniafort . . . de poenitentia et matrimonio cum glossis Joannis Fribergo* (Romae, 1603). The gloss in this edition is actually the work of Gulielmus Redonensis, written around 1250. Cf. Schulte, *Die Geschichte der Quellen und Literatur des canonischen Rechts von Gratian bis auf die Gegenwart* (3 vols., Stuttgart, 1875-1880), II, 413-414.

[29] S. Kuttner and B. Smalley, "The *Glossa Ordinaria* to the Gregorian Decretals," *The English Historical Review,* LX (1945), 97, 100.—*Glossa ordinaria* to the Decretals, in *Decretales D. Gregorii Papae IX . . . una cum glossis . . .* (Romae, 1582).

[30] Van Hove, *Prolegomena,* pp. 362, 477; Tierney, *Conciliar Theory,* p. 259.—*Commentaria in quinque libros decretalium* (Venetiis, 1570 [hereafter cited *Commentaria*]).

HOSTIENSIS (Henricus de Segusio): Known as the "*juris utriusque monarcha,*" Hostiensis rivals Innocent IV as a canonist. He studied at Bologna and taught at Paris before becoming chaplain to Pope Innocent. Hostiensis, so named because of his appointment as Cardinal Bishop of Ostia (1262), is remembered for two very influential commentaries on the Decretals of Gregory IX; a *Summa,* known as the *Summa aurea* (ca. 1250), and a voluminous *Lectura,* completed just before his death in 1271.[31]

GULIELMUS DURANTIS: Born in 1230 or 1231, Guilielmus was destined to become one of the most important canonists of the late thirteenth century. His *Speculum judiciale,* written around 1272, was one of the more influential of the many practical *Ordines judiciarii* which appeared in the thirteenth and fourteenth centuries. Also known as the *Speculator,* Gulielmus was made bishop of Mende in 1286, and died ten years later.[32]

GUIDO DE BAYSIO (Archidiaconus): Made archdeacon of Bologna in 1296, Guido was the compiler of the *Rosarium* (1300), an immense *Apparatus* of *glossae* on the *Decretum Gratiani,* and a commentary (1306-1311) on the *Liber Sextus* of Boniface VIII.[33]

JOANNES ANDREAE: Joannes Andreae was born about 1270. A layman, he was a pupil of Guido de Baysio, and taught at

[31] Van Hove, *Prolegomena,* pp. 476, 479; Tierney, *Conciliar Theory,* p. 259.—*Summa aurea* (Venetiis, 1570); *Commentaria in libros decretalium* (6 vols., Venetiis, 1581 [hereafter cited *Commentaria*]). The commentary on *Liber VI* of this 1581 edition of the *Lectura* is actually the commentary of Hostiensis on the *Novellae of* Innocent IV.

[32] Van Hove, *Prolegomena,* pp. 490-492; Tierney, *Conciliar Theory,* p. 258; L. Falletti, "Guillaume Durand," *Dictionnaire de droit canonique* (edd. A. Villien, E. Magnin, A. Amanieu, R. Naz, Paris, 1924-), cols. 1015-1017.—*Speculum juris Gulielmi Durandi* (4 vols., Venetiis, 1577). Also cited is the important liturgical work of Guilielmus, the *Rationale divinorum officiorum* (Venetiis, 1519).

[33] Van Hove, *Prolegomena,* pp. 475, 483-484.—*Rosarium seu in Decretorum volumen commentaria* (Venetiis, 1577); *In Sextum Decretalium commentaria* (Venetiis, 1577).

Padua, then at Bologna until his death in 1348. He produced several canonical works, among them the *Glossa ordinaria* on the *Liber Sextus,* written before the death of Boniface VIII in 1303, and the *Glossa ordinaria* on the *Clementinae.*[34]

C. Later Canonists

Commentaries of the following canonists who wrote after Joannes Andreae are cited in this study: HENRICUS DE BOHIC (d. 1350), a native of Brittany who lectured at Paris;[35] AEGIDIUS DE BELLAMERA (d. 1407);[36] and PANORMITANUS (Nicholas de Teduschis, 1386-1445), who Le Bras believes gives "a clear picture of the state of the law and and of canonistic science at the very close of the Middle Ages."[37]

ARTICLE 2. A NOTE ON MEDIEVAL CONCEPTS OF ECCLESIASTICAL JURISDICTION

Some understanding of the medieval canonists' concepts of ecclesiastical authority is necessary in order to appreciate their opinions regarding the juridic status of the layman. The precise terminology employed by the Code of Canon Law and the present-day canonists to describe and explain the Church's power to teach, to rule, and to sanctify her members did not exist in the twelfth and thirteenth centuries. Yet this was the period in which the speculative foundations were laid for the unambiguous distinctions and definitions we now possess. Typical of this activity was

[34] Van Hove, *Prolegomena,* pp. 474-475.—*Glossa ordinaria* to the *Liber Sextus,* in *Liber Sextus Decretalium D. Bonifacii VIII . . .* (Romae, 1582).

[35] Van Hove, *Prolegomena,* p. 495.—*Henrici Boich . . . in quinque decretalium libros commentaria* (Venetiis, 1576).

[36] Van Hove, *Prolegomena,* p. 496.—*In decretales libros praelectiones* (6 vols., Lugduni, 1548-1549).

[37] "Canon Law," p. 328. The dates are those of Lefebvre in the article "Panormitain," *Dictionnaire de droit canoique,* Fasc. XXXV (1957), 1195.—*Commentaria in quinque libros decretalium* (5 vols. in 7, Venetiis, 1588).

the gradual clarification by the canonists of the distinction between ecclesiastical jurisdiction and the power of orders.

The word *jurisdictio* appears only rarely in the ecclesiastical writers prior to Gratian. Pope Gregory the Great (590-604) was probably the first to borrow the word from Roman Law. He seems to have used it in both the classical sense of *potestas juris dicendi,* and as a synonym for the more general *potestas regendi,* a meaning found in the post-classical Roman Law.[38] From the seventh to the twelfth century, however, *jurisdictio* usually had only the more generic connotation of public authority when it appeared in papal documents. It was infrequently used.[39]

Gratian used the word *jurisdictio* at least twice in addition to its incorporation in the canons of the *Decretum.* It certainly has the generic sense of *potestas* or *auctoritas* in the rubric which reads: "Apostolica auctoritas a jurisdictione Archiepiscopi Episcopos valet eximere."[40] For the canon which this rubric introduces is taken from a letter of Pope Gregory I in which *jurisdictio* has the wider meaning.[41] The other reference, however, finds the word with the more restricted meaning of judicial jurisdiction.[42]

[38] In the classical Roman Law, *jurisdictio* (from *jus dicere*) referred only to the judicial activity of the magistrates and imperial officials, particularly that of the praetor during the *in jure* stage of a civil trial. Gradually the word took on a wider meaning. The power of the magistrate became known as his *jurisdictio,* the same term being applied to the territory within which that power could be exercised. In later times, the *jurisdictio* of the provincial governor referred to his entire administration of the province.—*Berger, Encyclopedic Dictionary of Roman Law,* Vol. XLIII, pt. 2 of *Transactions of the American Philosophical Society* (Philadelphia, 1953), p. 523, s.v. *Jurisdictio.*

[39] Tirado, *De jurisdictionis acceptatione in jure ecclesiastico* (Romae: Collegium Internationale ss. Teresia a Jesu et Joannis a Cruce, 1940), p. 29.

[40] C. XVI, q. 1, c. 52 (rubric).

[41] Reg., III, Ep. 7—*Monumenta Germaniae Historica* (188 vols., incomplete, Hannoverae, 1826 [hereafter cited *MGH*], *Epistolarum sectio II* (7 toms., edd. P. Ewald and M. Hartmann, 1887-1928), I, 167.

[42] C. XIII, q. 2, c. 6 (dictum): "Si quis de provincia ad provinciam

The early Decretists gave *jurisdictio* a variety of meanings. Rufinus, for example, while recognizing the classical meaning of the word,[43] used it to describe the general authority of the bishop over his subjects,[44] and also his power to punish.[45]

Although the term *jurisdictio* was not often used in their works, Gratian and the early Decretists were not without words with which to describe the Church's *potestas regiminis*. Gratian used as synonyms for this power *auctoritas*,[46] *potestas*,[47] and the phrase *regendi et jubendi potestas*.[48] In the Glossators of the period one finds such expressions as *jus et dominium episcopi, jus diocesanum, lex diocesana, populum sibi subjectum habere, lex jurisdictionis*, and *potestas ligandi et solvendi* used to express ecclesiastical jurisdiction in this general sense.[49]

It was during the twelfth century that the first scientific efforts were made to define and distinguish the more important elements in the concept of public ecclesiastical authority. This period saw a great development in speculative Theology as well as in Canon Law; and both movements demanded a more exact terminology in regard to the powers of the Church. The canonists contributed their share of distinctions. Gratian, for example, used the phrase *potestas ligandi et solvendi* to express both the power to forgive sins and the papal authority in judicial matters. This gave the Decretists an opportunity to theorize about the two elements needed for the valid conferment of absolu-

transiret, et ibi domicilium sibi collocaret . . . jurisdictioni illius judicis subiiceretur, in cuius provincia sedem sibi eligeret . . ."; cf. Tirado, *op. cit.*, pp. 64-67.

[43] *Summa*, at C. XI, q. 1, c. 5 (Singer, p. 310).

[44] *Summa*, at C. XVI, q. 1, c. 52 (Singer, p. 356).

[45] *Summa*, at D. LXIII, c. 22 (Singer, p. 157).

[46] D. XCVI, c. 10 (rubric).

[47] C. X., q. 1, cc. 2-7.

[48] D. XXI, c. 3 (dictum).

[49] Van de Kerckhove, "De notione jurisdictionis apud Decretistas et priores Decretalistas," *Jus Pontificium*, XVIII (1938), 11, n. 3.

tion, namely sacramental power and jurisdictional authority.[50]

Among the Glossators, Rufinus carefully distinguished between a bishop's *auctoritas* and his *potestas administrationis.* For him the distinction between orders and jurisdiction was not clear, the full *auctoritas* coming with, and being dependent upon, episcopal consecration.[51] Later in the century the distinction between orders and jurisdiction became more explicit in canonical writings. Thus Huguccio (ca. 1190) pointed out that the Apostles were equal to Peter in the possession of orders; not, however, in *jurisdictio* and *administratio.*[52]

Sometime between 1215 and 1250 *jurisdictio* became the common term by which the canonists expressed the public power of the Church to rule and govern, though it was also used in the strict sense of judicial jurisdiction. This power

[50] Compare C. XXIV, q. 1, c. 4 (dictum) and D. XX, c. 1 (dictum). For detailed treatment of this, see Tierney, *Conciliar Theory,* pp. 31 ff.; Ancieux, *La théologie du sacrement de pénitence au XIIe siècle,* Universitas Catholica Lovaniensis Dissertatione ad gradum magistri in Facultate Theologica vel in Facultate Juris Canonici consequendum conscriptae, Series II, Tomus 41 (Louvain: E. Nauwelaerts, 1949), pp. 303-310; 548 ff.

[51] Regarding the status of a bishop-elect prior to consecration he says: "dicimus quod plenam potestatem habeat quoad administrationem, non autem quoad dignitas auctoritatem, et ideo jure plene administrationis potest aliquos ab administratione procurationum vel ordinum suspendere... Deponere autem... non potest qui plenitudinem auctoritatis nondum habet, quam ex sola consecratione est certissimum evenire."—*Summa,* at D. XXIII, c. 1 (Singer, p. 52); cf. *Summa* at D. XXI, c. 1 (Singer, p. 47), and below, p. 70. Nor are the two powers separated in the definition he attempted of this general authority of the bishop, the *lex diocesana*: "est autem lex diocesana, qua episcopus potestatem habet dispensandi spiritualia et ministros instituendi et ordinandi, et visitandi et quartam exigendi in sua parochia catedraticam..."—*Summa,* at C. X., q. 1, c. 1 (Singer, p. 301).

[52] *Summa,* at C. XXI, *ante* c. 1, as given by Tierney, *op. cit.,* p. 33: "... illi pares fuerunt quo ad ordinem, quia quecumque ordines habuit Petrus habuit et quilibet aliorum sed Petrus prefuit illis in dignitate prelationis, in administratione, in jurisdictione...."

was carefully distinguished from that of orders..[53] Also, acts of ordinary temporal administration were distinguished from the exercise of jurisdiction by this time.[54]

Because the medieval writers were slow to develop clear definitions of the Church's powers, a study of the views of the canonists regarding the possession of ecclesiastical authority by laymen can be undertaken only with a certain amount of caution. The confusion of concepts which existed during the period makes it difficult to determine, in every case, the kind and degree of authority individual canonists had in mind when discussing the layman. Context often fails to serve as a reliable guide. And the time at which the canonist in question wrote, while an important factor, does not always point to a solution of this problem, especially since the later canonists frequently only repeated the views—and the obscure terminology—of their predecessors. The situation is further complicated by the fact that citation of an earlier writer as taking a particular position can usually be taken to mean only that the Decretist or Decretalist quoted was considered an authority, and not that he was the originator of the opinion.[55]

[53] Compare, for example, the confusing definition of Joannes Teutonicus (ca. 1215) in the *Glossa ordinaria* on C. X, q. 1, c. 1, s.v. *quidem laicus*: "lex jurisdictionis est qua episcopus potest clericos ordinare, altaria et ecclesias et virgines consecrare, corrigere, suspendere, cognoscere de causis civilibus et criminalibus et generaliter ad suum jurisdictionem pertinent omnia sacramenta conferre," with the later statement of Bernard of Parma: "... Electus, confirmatus, non consecratus potest exercere quae sunt jurisdictionis, non autem ea quae sunt ordinis episcopalis."—*Glossa ordinaria* on X, I, 6, c. 15.

[54] Van de Kerckhove, "De notione jurisdictionis apud Decretistas et priores Decretalistas," pp. 12-14; Heintschel, *The Medieval Concept of an Ecclesiastical Office*, The Catholic University of America Canon Law Studies, n. 363 (Washington, D.C.: The Catholic University of America Press, 1956), pp. 14-15. Cf. Tirado, *op. cit.*, pp. 88-102 for a number of definitions of jurisdiction offered by thirteenth and fourteenth century canonists.

[55] "Medieval doctrine should be viewed like rivers into which tributaries, large and small, empty their water. Definite attributions can never be made without a thorough study of the whole line of

A number of difficulties of this kind have been encountered in the preparation of this dissertation; some of them are apparently insolvable. Because of the limited sources at hand, the writer has felt justified in not attempting to disentangle every intricate problem of terminology which has presented itself. The presentation of even the less clear passages of the canonists regarding the layman, however, should be of some usefulness in understanding the attitude of the canonists toward his status. Future research in medieval canonical literature may provide the key to a clarification of many of these obscurities.

tradition. Any one familiar with the methods of the glossators and with the often arbitrary transmission of their sigla, will always be on guard against identifying a master as the originator of a doctrine on the mere strength of the fact that he is explicitly named in a gloss as holding this doctrine."—Stickler, "Concerning the Political Theories of the Medieval Canonists," p. 456.

CHAPTER TWO

THE CONCEPTS OF CLERGY AND LAITY IN MEDIEVAL CANONICAL WRITING

A study of the layman's canonical status demands some presentation of the concept the canonists had of the layman as distinct from the clergy and from the religious. The writings of the medieval canonists are filled with references to the cleric and the layman, to such an extent in fact that one is inclined to become discouraged when faced with the task of unraveling the various meanings of the words *clericus* and *laicus* in the variety of contexts in which they occur.[1] At the risk of oversimplification of a complicated subject, this chapter attempts a brief analysis of the general concept of clergy and laity had by the canonists whose works are under consideration. The first article examines the canonical concept of clergy and laity in the text of the *Decretum* most frequently cited by the canonists to point to the existence of these two states in the Church. The second illustrates, by way of examples, the more important senses in which the canonists employed the terms *clericus* and *laicus,* and compares these usages with those of the Code of Canon Law. A final article studies the attitude of the canonists toward the ceremony of first tonsure, which historically brought about the extension of the juridic clerical state to include those not in orders.

[1] Ullmann remarks of the word *cleric* that "anyone acquainted with medieval society knows the vagueness of the term"—*Medieval Papalism, The Political Theories of the Medieval Canonists,* The Maitland Memorial Lectures, Lent Term, 1948 (London: Methuen and Co., 1949), p. 95; but cf. the criticism of this view by Stickler, "Concerning the Political Theories of the Medieval Canonists," p. 456.

ARTICLE 1. THE TWO CLASSES OF CHRISTIANS

Without hesitation it can be said that one text in the *Decretum* of Gratian was considered by his followers to contain the basic teaching of the *Magister* on the nature of the distinction between cleric and layman. That this canon influenced considerably their own thought on the status of laymen in particular is apparent from the fact that it was usually cited by the canonists when discussing any question involving the rights or the obligations of laymen.

The canon in question, which hereafter will be referred to by its opening words, *Duo sunt genera,* is found among the canons of *Causa XII.* Gratian devoted the first Question of this *Causa* to a discussion of ownership of temporal goods by clerics. Among the canons he cited as arguing against such possession is the following:

> Duo sunt genera Christianorum. Est autem genus unum, quod mancipatum divino offitio, et deditum contemplationi et orationi, ab omni strepitu temporalium cessare convenit, ut sunt clerici, et Deo devoti, videlicet conversi. Κλῆρος enim grece latine sors. Inde huiusmodi homines vocantur clerici, id est sorte electi. Omnes enim Deus in suos elegit. Hi namque sunt reges, id est se et alios regentes in virtutibus, et ita in Deo regnum habent. Et hoc designat corona in capite. Hanc coronam habent ab institutione Romanae ecclesiae in signo regni, quod in Christo expectatur. Rasio vero capitis est temporalium omnium depositio. Illi enim victu et vestitu contenti nullam inter se proprietatem habentes, debent habere omnia communia. Aliud vero est genus Christianorum, ut sunt laici. Λαός enim est populus. His licet temporalia possidere, sed non nisi ad usum. Nichil enim miserius est quam propter nummum Deum contempnere. His concessum est uxorem ducere, terram colere, inter virum et virum judicare, causas agere, oblationes super altaria ponere, decimas reddere, et ita salvari poterunt, si vicia tamen benefaciendo evitaverint.[2]

[2] C. XII, q. 1, c. 7.

Gratian titled this canon as a letter of St. Jerome, as he says, "ad quendam suum Levitam, de duobus generibus hominum." The text is actually of much later origin. Berardi believes it to have been the work of an unknown writer of the eleventh or twelfth century.[3] But whatever its origin, the canon takes its importance for our purposes by reason of its incorporation here in the fundamental textbook of the canonists. Its etymological and descriptive definitions of the clerical and lay states will now be examined in greater detail.

The canon *Duo sunt genera* contains etymological definitions of both *clericus* and *laicus*. Of the former we read:

> Κλῆρος grece latine sors. Inde huiusmodi homines vocantur clerici, id est sorte electi. Omnes enim Deus in suos elegit.

Earlier in the *Decretum*, Gratian had placed a text from St. Isidore's *Etymologies*, containing both this opinion, shared by St. Jerome, and the view of St. Augustine that the Christian usage of the word was prompted by the choice of the Apostle Matthias by means of the casting of lots.[4] Both these definitions are consistent with the classical and Scriptural usages of Κλῆρος.[5]

[3] *Gratiani canones genuini ab apocryphis discreti* (4 vols., Venetiis: Ex Typographia Petri Valvensis, 1777), III, 157.

[4] *Acts of the Apostles,* 1: 15-26. "Cleros et clericos hinc appellatos credimus, quia Mathias sorte electus est, quem primum per apostolos legimus ordinatum. Κλῆρος enim grece, latine sors vel hereditas dicitur. Propterea ergo sunt clerici, quia de sorte Domini, vel quia Domini partem habent."—D. XXI, c. 1; St. Isidore, *Etymolog.*, VII, 12, in Migne, *Patrologiae cursus completus, series latina* (221 vols., Parisiis, 1844-1855), LXXXII, 290-291 (hereafter cited *MPL*). "Vocantur Clerici, vel quia de sorte sunt Domini, vel quia ipse Dominus sors, id est, pars clericorum est..."—St. Jerome, *Ep. 7 ad Nepotianum* (*MPL*, XXII, 531); C. XII, q. 1, c. 5. "Nam et Cleros et Clericos hinc appellatos puto, qui sunt in ecclesiastici ministerii gradibus ordinati, quia Matthias sorte electus est, quem primum per Apostolos legimus ordinatum"—St. Augustine, *Enarrationes in Psalmos*, LXVII, 19 (*MPL*, XXXVI, 824).

[5] Κλῆρος or Κλᾶρος had several meanings in classical Greek, among them *lot* and *that which is assigned by lot or allotment.* In

For the etymology of *laicus*, our canon has simply:

> Aliud vero est genus Christianorum, ut sunt laici. Λαός enim est populus.

The placing of λαός in opposition to κλῆρος, as in the context here, is a usage differing from that of Sacred Scripture. In the Old Testament, λαός (populus) referred principally to the Jews as the people of God, in contradistinction to the gentiles, a meaning found also in the New Testament.[6] Quite naturally the first Christians used the word to distinguish themselves from non-Christians.[7] Christian writers, however, began early to use the term also in opposition to Κλῆρὸς, and by the beginning of the third century this usage had become universal.[8]

The canonists also made mention of another etymological meaning of *laicus*, namely, that of a stone.[9] Thus Guido de Baysio attributed to Huguccio the opinion: "... populus, alibi laos, lapis interpretatur; inde laicus, id est, popularis

the Septuagint it was used in reference to the Levites, e.g., at Deuteronomy, 18: 2, Κύριος αὐτὸς Κλῆρος αὐτοῦ. Cf. *A Greek-English Lexicon*, ed. Henry Liddell, Robert Scott et al. (9. ed., Oxford: Clarendon Press, 1942), p. 959.

[6] E.g., *Exodus*, 19: 4-7; *Deuteronomy*, 7: 6-12; *Matthew*, 2: 6. As a substantive, λαϊκός is not found in the Bible; but λαός, the adjective of which is λαϊκός, occurs frequently—Congar, *Lay People in the Church* (trans. D. Attwater, Westminster, Md.: Newman Press, 1957), p. 1. Classical Greek meanings were many, including *men, soldiers, the civil population,* and also *the common men as opposed to their leaders*—*A Greek-English Lexicon*, p. 1029.

[7] E.g., *II Corinthians*, 9: 23.

[8] Congar, *op. cit.*, p. 2. St. Clement of Rome first distinguished λαϊκός, the layman, from the members of the hierachy. "Special functions are assigned to the high priest; a special office is imposed upon the priests; and special ministrations fall to the Levites. The layman is bound by the rules laid down for the laity."—*Epistle to the Corinthians*, 40, 5, as translated by James Kleist in *Ancient Christian Writers* (J. Quasten and J. Plumpe, eds., Westminster, Md.: The Newman Press, 1949-), I, 34. Kleist notes (p. 112) that this is the first time λαϊκός appears for *layman* in Christian literature.

[9] Derived from λαός, the genitive of λᾶας, *a stone*—*A Greek-English Lexicon*, p. 1029.

vel lapideus respectu clerici."[10] The reference here is no doubt to the layman as a member of the unlettered class, a common enough identification in medieval times. Gratian himself seems to have considered the cleric as a *homo literatus,* and similar expressions can be found in other canonistic writing.[11]

Taken by themselves, the etymological definitions of the canon *Duo sunt genera* point only to the distinction between the Church's rulers and ministers, her clerics, and those of the faithful who have no special calling to the service of the Church. The remainder of the canon, however, presents an entirely different picture. For here the distinction between the two Christian states rests not upon official function, but upon vocation to a life of perfection. It is the life of those not of this world contrasted with the life of the people in the world.

> Est autem genus unum quod mancipatum divino offitio, et deditum contemplationi et orationi, ab omni strepitu temporalium cessare convenit. . . . Aliud vero est genus Christianorum, ut sunt laici.[12]

This comparison illustrates a tendency in the medieval Church to classify the people into two segments rather than three. In the third and fourth centuries the clerical, monastic, and lay states were clearly distinguished one from the other. Gradually, however, the close relationship existing between the life of the cleric, who was chosen as the Lord's

[10] *Rosarium,* at C. XII, q. 1, c. 7, s.v. *Aliud.* The opinion: "Laicus, id est Lapideus; quia durus et extraneus a scientia literarum," is attributed to a contemporary of Guido, the Dominican Joannes of Genoa (ca. 1286)—Du Cange, *Glossarum mediae et infimae latinitatis* (ed. nova aucta . . . a Leopold Favre [1. ed., 1678-1736], 10 vols., Paris, 1937-1938), V, pp. 14-15, s.v. *Laicus.*

[11] D. LXXXVIII, c. 8, where Gratian substituted *clericus* in the rubric for *homo literatus* in the text. About a prohibition of lay participation in theological disputes, Joannes Andreae noted: "Forte intellexerunt de laico ad modum ultramontanorum, qui illiteratos vocant, et literatos clericos vocant"—*Glossa ordinaria* on VI°, V, 2, c. 2, s.v. *Laicae.* For the equation of *laicus* and *idiota,* an illiterate, uncultivated man, see Congar, *op. cit.,* p. 1.

[12] C. XII, q. 1, c. 7, "Duo sunt genera. . . ."

portion, and that of the monk, who chose the Lord as his portion, brought about a fusion of the two concepts, particularly when compared with a third concept, that of the layman in the world. Various reasons have been brought forth to explain this phenomenon. It was fitting that clerics have a monastic spirituality; and the practice of their living monastically did spring up in the West. Again, the liturgical way of life that was a characteristic of western monasteries brought about the practice of monks themselves becoming clerics and receiving ordination. This does not mean, of course, that the fundamental differences between clerics and monks was ever lost sight of.[13]

The hierarchy described in the canon *Duo sunt genera* is, then, one of virtue rather than of regimen: "Hi namque sunt reges, id est se et alios regentes in virtutibus." The possibility of salvation for the laity is mentioned as if it were a concession: ".... et ita salvari poterunt, si vicia tamen benefaciendo evitaverint." The lay state is defined in a negative way, by contrasting the layman's activities with the life of the cleric and the religious. The layman is allowed to marry and possess temporal goods. His work is to till the soil rather than to care for souls and contemplate spiritual things. He can settle men's legal disputes, so long as they do not involve the privilege of clerical immunity. He is to make offerings and pay tithes, an obligation not incumbent on the clergy and religious.[14]

In view of the variety of description contained in the canon *Duo sunt genera,* and the possible ways of interpreting it, we have now to look for the principal reason for its very frequent citation by the canonists. The canon does not seem to take its importance from the etymological definitions it contains. Neither was it of any great value to the canonists for its general description of the respective duties of cleric and layman, although the passive role

[13] Congar, *op. cit.*, p. 307 for the substance of this paragraph.

[14] "His concessum est uxorem ducere, terram colere, inter virum et virum judicare, causas agere, oblationes super altaria ponere, decimas reddere..."—C. XII, q. 1, c. 7.

it gave the layman in ecclesiastical affairs would also be assigned him by the later canonists. Certainly the canon's passing reference to possession or non-possession of temporal goods was not of particular interest, for this canon occupied a relatively insignificant place in a Question devoted entirely to this subject.

In the writer's opinion, the fact that this canon was usually cited by the canonists when denying laymen ecclesiastical authority in one or the other area is the key to an understanding of its importance. Gratian here provided the canonists with a legal basis—if not in legislation, at least in their fundamental legal text—to support a strict juridic dichotomy between cleric and layman, and therefore between their respective rights and obligations. To this dichotomy they would appeal time and again when faced with the very real challenge of defending the rights of the Church against the excesses of lay rulers, from emperor down to the master of the smallest estate. What some of these abuses were, and how the attitude of the canonists toward the layman's status was colored by their efforts to cope with them, is the subject matter of the next two chapters. It suffices to remark here that the followers of Gratian were not interested in the ascetical value of his definition, but in the fact that the writing of their *Magister* contained the statement: "Duo sunt genera hominum."

It is of interest to see how one later canonist looked upon the canon *Duo sunt genera*. For Hostiensis, the distinction contained therein was one between religious and layman rather than cleric and layman. The secular clergy he believed formed a third, middle group. Nevertheless, Hostiensis frequently cited the canon *Duo sunt genera* when defending the rights of the clergy.[15]

[15] "Ex praemissis patet fore duo genera hominum, scilicet laicorum, et religiosorum. Et duo genera vitarum, scilicet contemplativae et activae. Et duo genera scientiarum divinae scilicet et civilis, et hoc respicit decretum . . . (i.e., C. XII, q. 1, c. 7) . . . Sed sine dubio, addere possumus tertium genus, ex ingenio, quasi permixtum, nos enim clerici seculares, quos oportet domino famulari, et etiam curare ne

The concept of clergy and laity as comprising two separate Christian states is also present in the canonists' use of the word *ordo*.[16] When the word is applied to the lay state, or when *ordo clericalis* is contrasted with the *ordo laicalis,* it seems fairly safe to say that the canonists are referring to juridic states. For example, Gratian recorded the expression *ordo laicalis* at least twice in the more general sense of *status*.[17] And Stephen of Tournai compared the two classes of Christians in this manner: "Sicut laicorum ordine dignior est ordo clericorum. . . ."[18] But it is difficult to determine in every case whether *ordo* is being used to describe a class or a sacred power when such expressions as *ordo clericalis* and *ordo clericatus* occur in contexts dealing exclusively with the clerics.[19]

ARTICLE 2. COMPREHENSION OF THE TERMS *clericus* AND *laicus* AS USED BY THE MEDIEVAL CANONISTS

The Code of Canon Law defines clerics as those who

pereant possessiones ecclesiasticae, in medio istorum sumus positi, tamquam centrum, aliud est enim genus religiosorum, aliud clericorum."—*Summa aurea,* Prologue, 9-10.

[16] In Roman Law, *ordo* generally meant a sequence or a right order. Thus *ordo* in the law of successions, in which a group of successors are admitted to the inheritance, or the *ordo* in which citizens were called for public services. It was also used with reference to a group of persons (e.g., the Senate), a social class (e.g., *ordo equester*), and persons in subordinate services of the state (e.g., *ordo scribarum*). —Berger, *Encyclopedic Dictionary of Roman Law,* p. 612, s.v. *Ordo.*

[17] "Qui in laicali ordine consistunt . . ."—D. IV, c. 6, which is a spurious letter attributed to Pope Gregory the Great; Jaffe, *Regesta Pontificum Romanorum ab condita Ecclesia ad annum post Christum natum MCXVIII* (2. ed., correctam et auctam auspiciis Gulielmi Wattenbach, curaverunt, F. Kaltenbrunner, P. Ewald, S. Loewenfeld, 2 vols., Lipsiae, 1885-1888 [hereafter cited Jaffe]), n. 1987. Also at C. IV, q. 1, c. 2: "Excommunicati, sive ex clero sive ex laicali ordine . . ."—from a letter of Pope Nicholas I (ca. 865); Jaffe, n. 2796.

[18] *Summa,* at C. XXVI, *principium* (Schulte, p. 231). Cf. Rufinus: "Cum itaque laicis clericorum senatus premineat . . ."—*Summa,* at C. XXVII, *principium* (Singer, pp. 429-430).

[19] E.g., at X, I, 14, c. 11, where both expressions are used in a text relating to tonsure. Cf. below, p. 35.

have been attached to the divine ministry by the reception of first tonsure.[20] In giving this juridic definition, the Code makes no mention of the pre-Code practice of extending the meaning of *clericus, in materia favorabili,* to all religious, even novices, and of restricting it, *in materia odiosa,* to the members of the secular clergy who were not ecclesiastical dignitaries.[21] Since no such distinction is made, the word *clericus* is now to be understood in its proper meaning, unless another is apparent from the text or context.[22]

The most important instance of a broadening of the concept of *clericus* in the Code of Canon Law is found in canon 614, which extends to religious, even novices and lay religious, the four privileges of clerics mentioned in canons 119-123 (the *privilegium canonis, privilegium fori, privilegium immunitatis,* and the *privilegium competentiae*).[23] When the word *clericus* is used in these canons, then, it can be said to have, in law, a wider meaning than that found in canon 108, § 1; and this narrows the extension of *laicus* in a similar context.

The Code of Canon Law is not original in its retention of only these two meanings of *clericus* as the principal ones; for this was also the terminology of the medieval canonists. These meanings can easily be recognized as the more usual ones in their writings, although many times *clericus* and *laicus* appear in contexts where it is difficult to determine their exact extension.

The eleventh and twelfth centuries were periods in which more accurate descriptions were needed of the juridic differences between clerical and lay religious. As mentioned previously, the distinction between the cleric and the religious as such was never lost sight of in the history of the

[20] Can. 108, § 1: "Qui divinis ministeriis per primam saltem tonsuram mancipati sunt, clerici dicuntur."

[21] Vermeersch-Creusen, *Epitome juris canonici* (3 vols., Vol. I, 7. ed., 1949, Mechliniae-Romae: H. Dessain), I, n. 232.

[22] Cf. can. 18.

[23] Can. 614: "Religiosi, etiam laici, ac novitii, fruuntur clericorum privilegiis de quibus in can. 119-123."

Church, in spite of the tendency existing at times to consider them as one when compared with those "in the world." The canonists had over and above this constant tradition the explicit words of Gratian: "aliud enim convenit cuique ex eo, quod monachus est: aliud ex eo, quod clericus est."[24] From the end of the eleventh century, the further distinction between religious who were clerics and those who were not took on a new importance, for by this time the *conversi laici* had made their appearance as a new class of religious, during the Cluniac reform within the Benedictine congregations. These *conversi* were not monks, but laymen who helped with the farming and menial tasks around the monastery, and lived a religious life according to a rule first approved by Pope Calixtus II in 1119.[25]

The formation of the Knights Templars and the Hospitalers in connection with the Crusades also made necessary a clear juridic division between clerical and lay religious, for these military orders were composed almost entirely of laymen. Still later came the lay brothers attached to the Mendicant orders. The canonists would speak of all these groups as lay rather than as clerical religious.[26]

It was in connection with the extension of the privileges of clerics to those religious who were laymen that a wide

[24] C. XVI, q. 1, c. 40 (dictum). The distinction occurs repeatedly throughout this Question.

[25] Jaffe, n. 6795; Brockhaus, *Religious who are known as Conversi*, The Catholic University of America Canon Law Studies, n. 225 (Washintgon, D.C.: The Catholic University of America Press, 1956), p. 10. The lay brothers are called *conversi* here to distinguish them from the monks. Originally *conversi* described those who entered the monastery as adults rather than as young *oblati.* It was later applied to the *illiterati,* or *idiotae,* those monks who because of a belated vocation lacked any formal education, and therefore did not enter the clerical state. This is the sense in which *conversi* is used in C. XII, q. 1, c. 7, "Duo sunt genera..."; cf. Brockhaus, *op. cit.*, pp. 1-11.

[26] Guido de Baysio, for example, regarding the *conversi laici* forbidden to be present when clerical religious held elections: "etiam intelligimus templarios et hospitalarios... et fratres minores qui non sunt clerici"—*Commentaria,* at VI°, I, 6, c. 32, s.v. *conversi laici.*

use of the word *clericus* had its importance for the medieval canonists. In legislation incorporated in the *Decretum* one can occasionally find clerics and monks mentioned together in regard to these privileges. For example, a decree of the II Lateran Council (1139) was cited which included both clerics and monks as subjects of the *privilegium canonis*.[27] Later, the *conversi* received more specific mention as possessing these privileges, and the distinction between secular and religious *conversi* became more clear.[28] In matters involving ecclesiastical authority, however, the lay status of these religious was never left in doubt. Thus Innocent III wrote in 1199: "Nos attendentes, quod laicis, etiam religiosis, super ecclesiis et personis ecclesiasticis nulla sit attributa facultas. . . ."[29]

It should be mentioned here that the canonists looked upon the *conversi* and lay members of the military orders as *personae ecclesiasticae*. The expression seems to have been used frequently to describe all those who possessed clerical privileges and immunities. It appears to have had this meaning in the following passage from the *Decretum*.

[27] C. XVII, q. 4, c. 29 (*palea*), which is c. 15 of the Council as found in Mansi, *Sacrorum Conciliorum nova et amplissima collectio* (53 vols. in 60, Parisiis, 1901-1927 [hereafter cited Mansi]), XXI, 530. For the *privilegium fori*, see C. XI, q. 1, cc. 13, 14, 38.

[28] E.g., in a decretal of Pope Alexander III (1159-1181) at X, V, 39, c. 5: "qui violentas manus in clericos vel canonicos, aut cuiuslibet religionis conversos iniiciunt . . ."—Jaffe, n. 13893. Hostiensis commented at this point: "argumentum quod conversi secularium ecclesiarum non habent hoc privilegium. . . . Sed contra . . . iste non censetur omnino laicus, ergo censetur clericus quia duo sunt tantum hominum genera . . . Solutio: Aut est conversus remanens in domo propria et tanquam laicus vivens, et tunc non gaudet hoc privilegio, . . . Aut est conversus qui tradit se et sua, et est tonsuratus, . . . et vivit honeste, sicut et clericus vivere debet, et talis ex toto in forum ecclesiae intelligitur esse translatus, et immunitate ecclesiastica gaudere debet . . ."—*Commentaria*, at X, V, 39, c. 5, s.v. *religionis conversos*.

[29] X, I, 2, c. 10; Potthast, *Regesta Pontificum Romanorum inde ab anno post Christum natum MCXVIII ad annum MCCCIV* (2 vols., Berolini, 1874-1875 [hereafter cited Potthast]), n. 819. Boniface VIII: "In ecclesiis quoque regularibus, vel monasteriis . . . non debent . . . conversi laici cum clericis electionibus interesse"—VI°, I, 6, c. 32.

> Sacrilegium conmittitur, si quis infregerit ecclesiam... ; seu qui iniuriam vel ablationem rerum intulerit clericis arma non ferentibus, vel monachis, sive Deo devotis, omnibusque ecclesiasticis personis.[30]

Joannes Teutonicus enumerated as ecclesiastical persons: "... conversi et poenitentes, templarii, et hospitalarii, qui gaudent privilegio clericali."[31]

Religious women were not, of course, considered clerics in any strict sense of the word. Expressions such as *clerica nobilis, venerabilis clerica et honorabilis Priorissa,* and *potestas recipiendi moniales tam conversas quam clericas* appear in the literature of the period under study.[32] This is not surprising in an age which produced a phenomenon such as the mitered abbess. A separate article of this study will take up the canonists' views on the authority of religious superioresses.

It can be concluded that the medieval canonists made the same fundamental distinctions regarding the relations between the concepts of cleric, religious, and layman as those found in our present discipline. The juridic differences between clergy and laity, and between clerical and lay religious were clear to them. And while at times the word *clericus* was used or interpreted in a wide sense to include all religious, it was generally restricted, as it is today, to those who had entered the *status clericalis.* The areas of ecclesiastical authority forming the subject matter of this dissertation are such that the word will almost always have the more strict meaning when it appears in the quotations from the canonists' writings.

Article 3. The Teaching of the Canonists on the Nature of First Tonsure

The distinction between the clerical and lay states is

[30] C. XVII, q. 4, c. 21, attributed by Gratian to Pope John VIII (872-882); cf. Friedberg's note at this canon.

[31] *Glossa ordinaria* on C. XVII, q. 4, c. 21, s.v. *ecclesiasticis personis.*

[32] Cf. Du Cange, *Glossarum mediae et infimae latinatis,* II, 367.

fundamentally a divine one. The Council of Trent defined the divine origin of the hierarchical structure existing within the Church.[33] However, elements of both the divine law and the ecclesiastical positive law enter into our concepts of the clerical and lay states. These concepts have been affected considerably by centuries of positive legislation on the part of the Church. She has, for example, laid down certain prerequisites for admission to the clerical state, and granted to clerics a number of privileges and immunities. Both cleric and layman have been bound by a variety of obligations over and above those imposed by the divine law. Our concepts of these two states, therefore, are juridic as well as dogmatic.[34]

Because this study is concerned more with the layman's legal position than with his dogmatic status, it is of interest to consider what was the nature of first tonsure according to the canonists. For this ceremony marks the dividing line, so to speak, between the cleric and the layman; and it was by means of this institute that the Church extended the juridic clerical state to include subjects not possessed of the power of orders.

Theologians and canonists today agree that first tonsure is not one of the ecclesiastical orders properly so-called, but

[33] Sess. XXIII, cap. 4, *de sacramento ordinis*: "Si quis dixerit, in Ecclesia catholica non esse hierarchiam, divina ordinatione institutam, quae constat ex episcopis, presbyteris, et ministris: A.S."—*Enchiridion symbolorum definitionum et declarationum de rebus fidei et morum* (26. ed., edd. H. Denzinger, C. Bannwart, J. Umberg, Friburgi Brisgoviae: Herder and Co., 1946 [hereafter cited Denzinger]), n. 966.

[34] The word *status* essentially denotes a condition of being to which is attached some kind of permanence. St. Thomas Aquinas (1225-1274) described it as follows: "quandam positionis differentiam secundum quam aliquis disponitur secundum modum suae naturae, cum quadam immobilitate."—*Summa Theologica,* IIa IIae, q. 183, art. 1, c., in *Opera omnia* (34 vols., eds. S. Frettè et P. Marè, Parisiis: L. Vivès, 1871-1880), IV, 482. In Roman Law, the word generally indicated a legal condition, principally in relation to one's liberty, citizenship, or family position. See Berger, *Encyclopedic Dictionary of Roman Law*, p. 714.

a ceremony of initiation into the juridic clerical state. For several centuries, however, the nature of tonsure was heatedly debated, the theologian considering it to be only a ceremony with important juridic effects, the canonist believing it to be an order as well. The controversy came gradually to an end only after the Council of Trent had distinguished between tonsure and the minor orders in one of its dogmatic decrees.[35] The disagreement was typical of the debates between students of the two disciplines, particularly in the Later Middle Ages, with each side arguing from different principles, and each appealing to earlier members of their own schools as authorities to support their diverse conclusions.[36]

The monastic custom of wearing the tonsure was adopted by clerics toward the end of the fifth century or at the beginning of the sixth. The IV Council of Toledo (633) gave the first clear legislation on the wearing of tonsure by

[35] Sess. XXIII, cap. 2, *de sacramento ordinis*: "... ut in Ecclesia ordinatissima dispositione plures et diversi essent ministrorum ordines, qui sacerdotio ex officio deservirent, ita distributi, ut qui iam clericali tonsura insigniti essent, per minores ad maiores ascenderent..."—Denzinger, n. 958. Cf. Gasparri, *Tractatus canonicus de sacra ordinatione* (2 vols., Paris, 1893-1894), I, 16; Cappello, *Tractatus canonici-moralis de sacramentis*, 5 vols., Vol. IV, 3. ed., 1951, Romae: Marietti), IV, 71. A survival of the medieval notion that tonsure should be included under *ordo* can perhaps be found in Canon 950 of the Code of Canon Law, which reads: "In jure verba: *ordinare, ordo, ordinatio, sacra ordinatio,* comprehendunt, praeter consecrationem episcopalem, ordines enumeratos in can. 949 et ipsam primam tonsuram, nisi aliud ex natura rei vel ex contextu verborum eruatur."

[36] Fagnanus (1588-1678), whose immense commentary on this point might be called the canonists' "last stand" in defense of their traditional view, aptly described the debate, for him a "quaestio insignis": "Et quidem Theologi usque adeo suis rationibus et argumentis nituntur, ut ad statuta Canonum fere vix advertere videantur... E converso autem Canonistae suis Canonibus haerent tam fixe, et tenaciter, ut Theologorum ratiocinationes et objecta omnia videantur contemnere."—*Jus Canonicum seu Commentaria absolutissima in quinque decretalium libros* (3 vols., Venetiis, 1729), I, 418, at X, I, 14, c. 11.

clerics.[37] At this time the practice of having clerics without orders was unknown, the ceremony of tonsure taking place at the time first minor orders were given. Sometime near the end of the seventh century, however, the first ceremonial cutting of the hair was separated from the conferment of orders. The occasion for this was the practice which arose at this time of parents presenting their young boys to the bishop or the monastery for service to the Church. These children received the tonsure and wore the clerical garb as a sign of their dedication. The II Council of Nicea (787) made mention of this practice existing in the monasteries.[38] Sometime later tonsure was given to adults preparing for the reception of orders, though the date at which this practice began cannot be determined with certainty.[39] Nor is it known at what time all the privileges of the clerical state were granted to those who had received only tonsure, though certainly this had taken place by 1210.[40]

Gratian set the stage for the canonists' identification of tonsure as a minor order by incorporating in the *Decretum* a variety of lists of the ecclesiastical orders. In three of these, mention was made of the cantor, or psalmist, who functioned in the early Church.[41] The duties of the psalm-

[37] C. 41—Mansi, X, 630.

[38] C. 14—Mansi, XIII, 753; D. LXIX, c. 1.

[39] The Council of Meaux in 845 decreed: "Canonicorum autem, qui in parochiis tonsurantur, et erudiuntur, interdum etiam et ordinantur, sine auctoritate dignitas regalis in suum periculum non dignetur recipere . . ."—c. 58, as found in Mansi, XIV, 832.

[40] The date of the important decretal of Innocent III, analyzed below, p. 35. For the substance of this paragraph, see Tixeront, *Holy Orders and Ordination, A Study in the History of Dogma* (tr. by S. Raemers, St. Louis: Herder, 1928), pp. 133-136; Gasparri, *op. cit.*, I, 23; McBride, *Incardination and Excardination of Seculars*, The Catholic University of America Canon Law Studies, n. 145 (Washington, D.C.: The Catholic University of America Press, 1941), pp. 84-88.

[41] D. XXI, c. 1, from St. Isidore, *Etymolog.*, VII, 12—*MPL*, LXXXII, 290-291; D. XXV, c. 1, a canon of uncertain origin attributed to St. Isidore (cf. Berardi, *Gratiani canones*, III, 392 ff.); and C. XXVII, q. 1, c. 4, which is c. 4 of the Council of Trullo (692)—Mansi, XI, 943.

ist are described in one of these canons in the following manner:

> Ad psalmistam pertinet officium canendi, dicere benedictiones, laudes, sacrificium responsoria, et quicquid pertinet ad canendi peritiam.[42]

In two other enumerations of the orders, however, the cantor was not included. These listed only eight orders, the four minor orders as we know them today, and the subdiaconate, diaconate, priesthood and episcopate.[43]

Gratian also recorded a canon of the III Council of Carthage (397), in which psalmists were considered clerics,[44] and a canon from the fifth century collection, the *Statuta ecclesiae antiqua,* which allowed psalmists to undertake their office of chanting without episcopal permission, provided a ceremony took place in which the priest said to the candidate: "Vide, ut quod ore cantas, corde credas, et quod corde credis, operibus comprobis."[45]

The early Decretists were not inclined to consider the *psalmistatus* as an order existing in the Church of their day. The references to the psalmist in the *Decretum* were believed to pertain only to an order of earlier times.[46] At

[42] D. XXV, c. 1.

[43] D. LXXVII, c. 1, a Pseudo-Isidorian letter attributed by Gratian to Pope Gelasius (492-496), and by Pseudo-Isidore to Pope Gaius (283-296)—Hinschius, *Decretales Pseudo-Isidorianae et Capitula Angilramni* (Lipsiae, 1863), p. 218; D. XCIII, c. 5, which is c. 7 of a council supposedly held in 324 by Pope Sylvester I, actually a part of the Symmachian forgeries incorporated into Pseudo-Isidore—See Hinschius, *op. cit.*, pp. 449-451; Mansi, II, 626.

[44] "Clericorum autem nomen etiam lectores et psalmistae hostiarii retinent."—D. LXXII, c. 2, which is c. 21 of the Council as found in Bruns, *Canones Apostolorum et Conciliorum saeculorum IV-VII* (2 vols., Berolini: G. Remerius, 1839 [hereafter cited Bruns]), I, 126.

[45] D. XXIII, c. 20, which is c. 10 of the *Statuta* as given in Bruns, I, 142. The rite of making a psalmist can still be found in Part III of the Roman Pontifical. There the form reads: "Vide, ut quod ore cantas, corde credas, et quod corde credis, operibus comprobes."—*Pontificale Romanum in tres partes distributum* (3 vols., Parisiis: J. Leroux et Jouby, 1852), II, 435.

[46] "Ordinem istum hodie non habemus."—Stephen of Tournai, *Summa,* at D. XXV, c. 1, s.v. *ad psalmistatam* (Schulte, p. 37). See also

least one Decretist, however, the unknown author of the *Summa Parisiensis,* believed that the *psalmistatus* could still be found in the Church, not as an order, but as a ceremony. He identified the psalmist as one who possessed tonsure without minor orders.

> Psalmista, i.e., cantor. Idem est qui videlicet coronam sine ordine habet, quem poterat quondam sacedotes ordinare, i.e., coronare.[47]

Early in the thirteenth century, a decretal letter of Pope Innocent III, later to be included among the official Decretals of Gregory IX, gave the canonists occasion to go contrary to the position of the early Decretists, and to recognize first tonsure as one of the ecclesiastical orders. In 1210 Innocent was asked by the Archbishop of Rouen whether or not the *ordo clericatus* was conferred when abbots tonsured their subjects. The Pope's reply took this form:

> Cum contingat interdum, quod laici, ad monasteria convolantes, a suis abbatibus tonsurentur, requisisti an clericatus ordo in tonsura hujusmodi conferatur. Super quo tibi respondemus, quod, cum in septima synodo sit statutum, ut lectores per manus impositionem licentia sit unicuique abbati . . . faciendi . . . per primam tonsuram, juxta formam Ecclesiae datam, a talibus clericalis ordo confertur.[48]

In the writer's opinion, the *ordo clericalis* or *clericatus* here is nothing more than a reference to the clerical state in general, the Archbishop's question being but to determine whether one became a cleric by monastic tonsure. Because of the ambiguous nature of the Latin word *ordo,* however,[49]

the *Summa Parisiensis* at the same place (McLaughlin, p. 25). Rufinus had no comment regarding the references in the Decretum to the *psalmista.*

[47] *Summa Paris.,* at D. XXIII, c. 20, s.v. *Psalmista* (McLaughlin, p. 24); also at D. XXI, c. 1, s.v. *psalmistae* (McLaughlin, p. 21), where the author notes that the ceremony by which one became a cantor was one reserved in his day to the bishop.

[48] X, I, 14, c. 11; Potthast, n. 4072. "In septima synodo" refers to c. 7 of the II Council of Nicea (787)—Mansi, XIII, 753.

[49] Noted above, p. 26.

the canonists interpreted the *ordo clericatus* in the more strict sense of a spiritual power conferred by ordination.[50]

Joannes Teutonicus was perhaps the first canonist to identify first tonsure as an ecclesiastical order. Commenting on the decretal of Innocent as it appeared in the *Compilatio Quarta,* he considered Innocent's response an explicit refutation of the earlier opinions of the Decretists.

> ...ordo, qui sic confertur, appellatur psalmistatus: tamen ubi agitur de singulis ordinibus [i.e., in the *Decretum*] nihil de hoc agitur... unde quidam dixerunt non esse ordinationem, sed eorum opinio corrigitur hic.[51]

For him the tonsure was a *sacramentale signum,* the reception of which made one a psalmist and a cleric.

> Hic patet, quod psalmista, et ostiarius, et lector sunt clerici... et qui iniicit manus in istos, excommunicatus est... et per primam tonsuram fit aliquis Psalmista, vel clericus, et illa tonsuram est sacramentale signum... tantum septem sunt ordines qui conferuntur cum solemnitate, sed tamen novem sunt.[52]

These views of Joannes Teutonicus were to become the more common teaching of the canonists on the nature of first tonsure. Joannes' gloss of Innocent's response was incorporated by Bernard of Parma in his gloss on the decretal as it appeared in the Decretals of Gregory IX.[53] Pope Innocent IV supported this opinion in his Commentary, but added that should the *psalmistatus* be omitted and the order

[50] Another ambiguity in the decretal was the expression *juxta formam Ecclesiae datam,* which later canonists would argue did not mean "given by the Church," as the theologians held, but rather "given to the Church," thus implying some kind of sacramental nature for the *ordo* as mentioned here. Cf. Fagnanus, *Jus Canonicum,* I, 421.

[51] *Glossa* on the *Compilatio Quarta,* I, 8, c. 1 (X, I, 14, c. 11). His contemporary, Vincentius Hispanus, considered the *psalmistatus* an order only in the wide sense, according to Guido de Baysio, *Rosarium,* at D. XXIII, c. 20.

[52] *Glossa ordinaria,* on D. XXI, c. 1, s.v. *Psalmista.* Cf. the glosses on D. LXIX, c. 1, s.v. *Lectoris,* and on C. XVII, q. 4, c. 29.

[53] *Glossa ordinaria,* on X, I, 14, c. 11, s.v. *clericalis ordo.*

of porter or lector given the candidate for ordination, there would be no need for the order of psalmist to be given, since no special *officium* was conferred by it.[54] Hostiensis also agreed with Joannes Teutonicus, but took exception to Innocent IV's view that no *officium* was conferred by the ceremony. For him the *psalmistatus* was a prerequisite to the reception of the other orders, a ceremony which initiated the candidate into the privileged ranks of the clergy. A definite *officium*, that of singing in the Church, was received through this important order.[55] This debate between Innocent and Hostiensis was frequently referred to by the later canonists.

It should be noted that the canonists did not overlook the juridic effects of first tonsure while arguing for its sacred character. This debate with the theologians was confined to the question of what tonsure was, rather than what effects it had in law.[56]

[54] "... sic apparet psalmistatum esse ordinem ... de hoc tamen ordine credimus quod si omittatur et conferatur vel lectoratus, vel ostiariatus, quod non est repetendum: sed si aliquis aliorum ordinum omittatur, recipiendus est. Ratio diversitatis est, quia in hoc ordine nullum officium speciale conceditur, sed in aliis sic, et recipiendo quemlibet aliorum ordinum videtur recepisse potestatem faciendi omnia, quae ad hunc ordinem pertinent."—*Commentaria*, at X, I, 14, c. 11, s.v. *ordo*.

[55] "Psalmistatus certus ordo est.... Et est principium et quasi fundamentum militiae clericalis, cui quis per hunc ordinem ascribitur.... Est enim certus ordo in ecclesia Dei.... Per quem recipit ordinatus officium cantandi in ecclesia Dei ...et per quem vinculum promovendi [recipit?], et ecclesiae quodammodo initiatur, et est privilegiatus ..."—*Commentaria*, at X, I, 14, c. 11, s.v. *cum contingat*. Durandus noted that many did not consider tonsure an order, but an *officium*.—*Rationale divinorum officiorum*, Lib. I, cap. 3. For the use of *officium* by the canonists in regard to the power of orders, cf. Heintschel, *The Medieval Concept of an Ecclesiastical Office*, Chs. II and III.

[56] Typical of the theologian's arguments to defend their views on the matter are these of St. Thomas Aquinas: Psalmistatus non est ordo ... quia non habet aliquam specialem relationem ad Eucharistiae Sacramentum."—*Comment.* in IV, dist. 24, q. 2, art. 1, *ad quintum*, in *Opera omnia*, XI, 36; "... quod corona habet interius aliquid spiri-

This indentification of tonsure as an ecclesiastical order could not but have its effect upon the concept that medieval canonists had of the layman's status. For them, the distinction between cleric and layman rested on something more than the wearing or not wearing of the clerical tonsure. It was based on something more fundamental, and more sacred, the distinction between the ordained and the unordained.

tuale quod ei respondet sicut signum signato; sed hoc non est aliqua spiritualis potestas; et ideo in corona non imprimitur character, nec est ordo . . ."—*Comment. in IV,* dist. 24, q. 3, art. 1, *ad primum,* in *Opera omnia,* XI, p. 40.

CHAPTER III

THE ATTACK OF THE MEDIEVAL CANONISTS UPON THE ABUSES OF THE PROPRIETARY CHURCH SYSTEM

The maxim that first impressions are often the most important has particular meaning when applied to the teaching of the medieval canonists regarding the status of the layman. For frequent repetition of the dicta of earlier canonists, and a continual appeal to the authority of the masters of the law was a characteristic of medieval canonical writing. The general stand taken by Gratian and the early Decretists on lay possession of ecclesiastical authority would quite naturally become the attitude of the canonists who followed them.

Unfortunately, the first juridic contact, so to speak, between the canonists and a body of laymen took place in connection with a number of serious abuses of the Church's authority on the part of the laymen. The purpose of this chapter is to show how the first canonists faced the problems these abuses presented to them, and by so doing to illustrate the negative character which the canonists' treatment of the status of laymen would have from the very beginnings of the science.

ARTICLE 1. HISTORICAL BACKGROUND

The teaching of Gratian and his early disciples on the proprietary church system cannot be fully appreciated without some understanding of the origin and development of the phenomenon of lay ownership of churches. For this reason it will not be out of place to present here by way of historical background a very brief account of the beginnings and rapid growth of the proprietary church, and of the efforts made by the Church to cope with the many problems arising from this institute.

The proprietary Church made its appearance in the history of the Church at the time of the invasion of the Germanic peoples. Private churches on the large Roman country estates were not unknown in the West before this time, but it was the Germanic concept of land tenure which was responsible for the medieval phenomenon of lay control of churches. The proprietary system was but the application to ecclesiastical property of the feudal principle that rights inhere in the land; that possession (*seizin*) of the land confers upon the possessor all the rights flowing from it. The concept of the Church as a moral person, as a subject capable of holding property, was foreign to such a concept. According to this principle, a chapel built by a lord upon his estate, or one already existing on land he had alienated, became the nucleus of a property complex, and everything connected with the church was considered but an adjunct to the land and the altar which stood upon it. The lord looked upon himself as complete master over the church, its furnishings, and its ministers. The rights which these laymen claimed for themselves became known as the *jus proprietarium*, *proprietas*, or simply *dominium*.[1]

It is easy to see how the clergy would come under the influence and power of the lay lords when such a system would be introduced in a diocese. The landowners considered the parish priest as their servant and reserved to themselves his appointment. The practice of having their own serfs ordained was a common abuse. They undertook phases of parochial administration heretofore reserved to

[1] Stutz, "The Proprietary Church as an Element of Mediaeval Germanic Ecclesiastical Law," *Studies in Mediaeval History* (ed. G. Barraclough, 2 vols., Oxford: Blackwell and Mott, 1938), II, 39-47; Thomas, *Le droit de propriété des laiques sur les églises et le patronage laïque au moyen age* (Paris, 1906), pp. 11-14, 19-28. Whether this private control of churches was the result of ancient Germanic traditions of worship or only the product of the evils of the age, such as lack of law enforcement, is disputed. See Thomas, *op. cit.*, pp. 28-33.

the clergy, and developed for themselves a number of profitable rights, among them the right to fees for the performance of baptisms, marriages, and funerals on their lands, and the right to share in the priest's private property when he died, the so-called *jus spolii.*[2]

Although proprietary churches were to be found in every region influenced by Germanic legal thought, the system was not equally effective in every land. But in the Frankish country, the proprietary church triumphed completely. Monasteries succumbed to this system of ownership. Gradually the baptismal churches and even the cathedrals became proprietary churches, with the bishop himself often in the position of feudal lord. In the ninth century the ecclesiastical benefice appeared, an institution which brought with it the abuse known as lay investiture. Entire bishoprics came to be considered proprietary holdings.[3]

Such a challenge to episcopal authority could not go unopposed by the Church. Legislation to eliminate lay control of churches appeared in several early councils, particularly in Visigothic Spain, where the encroachments of the lay lords were kept, comparatively speaking, to a minimum. as early as 511, the Council of Orleans decreed:

> Omnes autem basilicae quae per diversa loca constructae sunt vel cotidie construuntur, placuit secundum priorum canonum regulam, ut in eius episcopi, in cuius territorio sitae sunt, potestate consistant.[4]

The IV Council of Toledo (633) issued a strong affirmation of the bishop's authority over the churches in his diocese.[5]

[2] Stutz, "The Proprietary Church," pp. 52-53.

[3] For a short description of the complete breakdown of discipline in the tenth century Germany, see Hughes, *A History of the Church,* II, 199-201, 209 ff.

[4] C. 17, as found in Bruns, II, 164.

[5] "Noverint conditores basilicarum in rebus quas eisdem ecclesiis conferunt, nullam potestatem habere, sed juxta canonum constituta sicut ecclesiam, ita et dotem eius ad ordinationem episcopi pertinere." —c. 33, as found in Bruns, I, 233. A number of these early canons appear in the *Decretum,* and will be seen in connection with Gratian's teaching on the *jus patronatus.*

The continuous stream of legislation—much of it of Frankish origin—which appeared during the dark centuries between these councils and the Gregorian reform indicates the magnitude of these abuses, but at the same time testifies to the fact that the Church never officially sanctioned them.[6]

The proprietary church became so much a part of medieval life that not even the gigantic reform efforts of Pope Gregory VII were successful in eliminating all the abuses arising from it. Certainly Gregory recognized that bringing an end to every kind of private lordship over churches was a necessary objective of reform. However, he was also aware that he was not in a position to concentrate on both the major and minor churches at one time, because of the existing political situation. There was little chance that he could end all lay control of the lesser churches. On the other hand, conditions were more favorable to loose the hold which the King and the greater nobles had over the more important churches. For this reason, and perhaps because of the danger of driving the lay aristocracy into the camp of the king, Gregory's principal efforts were concentrated on ending the practice of lay investiture at the level of the bishopric.[7] This does not mean that any compromise or surrender of principles took place, for many of the Pope's reform canons were aimed at abuses involving all churches, both large and small. In spite of these efforts, and those of the I Lateran Council in 1123, enough abuse remained to justify Gratian and his followers taking up in some detail the problems of the proprietary system which had plagued the Church for centuries.

[6] A brief outline of this legislation is found in Kurtscheid, *Historia juris canonici, Historia institutorum ab Ecclesiae fundatione usque ad Gratianum* (Romae: Officium Libri Catholici, 1956), pp. 277-281. Thomas, *Le droit de propriété*, gives many excerpts from the councils of this period.

[7] This is the view of Stutz, "The Proprietary Church," pp. 66-68; cf. Feine, *Kirchliche Rechtsgeschichte*, I, 324.

Article 2. The Condemnation by Gratian and the Decretists of Lay Authority over Churches

Gratian devoted a series of canons in the *Decretum* to the many problems presented by the proprietary church system. The greater part of two Questions give excerpts from the Church's legislation aimed at bringing to an end the abuses which lay usurpation of ecclesiastical authority had produced in the past.[8]

Two fictitious cases introduce the Questions of the *Decretum* here under consideration. The first is at Causa X, where Gratian proposed the case of a certain layman who wished to separate a church he had built from the authority of the bishop. The bishop in turn claimed complete authority over the church, going so far as to seize it by force. Gratian then asked as his first Question: "an basilica cum omni dote sua ad episcopi ordinationem pertineat?"[9] The second case involved the possibility of a layman entrusting a church to the care of a monastery.[10] In answering these two questions, Gratian touched upon such subjects as the general authority of the bishop in parish affairs, the problem of lay investiture, and the possession and administration of tithes. By examining the rubrics and the dicta surrounding these canons, and by a study of the comments made upon them by several of the early Decretists, the attitude of the Church's first canonists toward the lay holders of churches can be discovered and evaluated.

Gratian replied to his first question with an uncompromising defense of the authority of the bishop over the churches in his territory. Consecrated churches could not be separated from the *lex diocesana.* To support this prin-

[8] C. X, q. 1, and C. XVI, q. 7. See also Stutz, "Gratian und die Eigenkirchen," *Zeitschrift der Savigny Stiftung für Rechtsgeschichte, Kanonistische Abteilung,* I (1911), pp. 1-33.

[9] C. X, *principium.*

[10] "... si laici capellam tenebant (ut quibusdam moris est) et in manibus abbatis eam refutaverint et ordinandam tradiderint, an consensu episcopi et clericorum abbas possit eam tenere?"—C. XVI, *principium.*

ciple he presented first a passage from the Council of Lerida, held in 546:

> Si ex laicis quisquam a se factam basilicam consecrari desiderat, nequaquam eam sub monasterii specie, ubi congregatio non colligitur, a diocesana lege audeat segregare.[11]

The reason underlying this canon was epitomized in the rubric: "Ecclesia et omnia jura earum ad episcopi ordinationem pertinent," which introduced another canon defending the bishop's rights over the churches.

> ...omnes ecclesiae cum dotibus suis, et decimis, et omnibus suis, in episcopi potestate consistant, atque ad ordinationem suam semper pertineant.[12]

For the most part, Gratian attacked the lay founder only indirectly, stressing the fact of the bishop's authority over the churches in his diocese. One rubric, however, explicitly excluded lay founders from any participation in this power: "Basilicarum conditores in rebus ecclesiarum nullam se potestatem habere cognoscant."[13]

It is to be noted that most of the legislation quoted by Gratian in defense of the bishop's authority was taken

[11] C. X, q. 1, c. 1, which is c. 3 of the council as found in Bruns, II, 21.

[12] C. X, q. 1, c. 3, taken from the spurious ninth century collection known as the *Capitularia Benedicti Levitae* (III [= VII], 468; *MPL*, XCVII, 860), in turn a paraphrase of c. 19 of the III Council of Toledo, held in 589 (Bruns, I, 217). Cf. E. Seckel, "Studien zu Benedictus Levita, VIII," *Zeitschrift der Savigny Stiftung für Rechtsgeschichte, Kanonistische Abteilung*, XXIV (1935), p. 70. Following the *Decretum* of Burchard (III, 146; *MPL*, CXL, 702) and the *Decretum* of Ivo of Chartres (III, 211; *MPL*, CLXI, 248), Gratian attributed the capitulary to a certain council of Chalon. Burchard habitually made royal capitularies, both genuine and spurious, appear as conciliar canons for apologetic reasons. Cf. Stickler, *Historia*, pp. 156-157. Among other pertinent rubrics of Gratian can be cited: "Omnes basilicae ad eum pertinent episocpum in cuius territorio positae sunt"—C. XVI, q. 7, c. 10; "Unaqueque parrochia episcopi provisione regatur"— C. X., q. 1, c. 4; "Judicio et potestate episcopi res ecclesiasticae gubernetur"—C. X, q. 1, c. 1.

[13] At C. X, q. 1, c. 6, introducing a canon of the IV Council of Toledo (633)—c. 33, Bruns, I, 233 (above p. 41).

from sixth and seventh century councils held in Gaul, and was originally directed against the lay founders of churches and their heirs. Keeping this in mind, as well as the fact that for Gratian the concepts of *lex diocesana, potestas,* and *ordinatio* connoted both jurisdictional and administrative power, we can conclude from an examination of these few quotations that the *Magister* conceded to lay holders of churches no authority whatsoever.

Though noted for their independence of judgment and for the variety of their opinions,[14] the early Decretists had little comment on the firm stand Gratian took against lay control of churches, other than to repeat the general principle that the bishop had complete authority over churches. Typical was the comment of Rolandus Bandinelli, the future Alexander III:

> Generaliter enim tam ecclesiae quam decimae nec non et quaelibet res ecclesiasticae in episcoporum et non laicorum consistunt. Laici enim nec decimas nec ecclesias sua vel alterius auctoritate possidere possunt.[15]

These early commentators were careful, however, to safeguard the rights of those monasteries exempted from the bishop's jurisdiction by special privilege of the Roman Pontiff.[16]

One of the more flagrant abuses of the proprietary system was the misappropriation of tithes and church funds by the lay lords. Gratian recorded in at least a dozen canons of the two Questions under study the Church's opposition to this practice, and in so doing strengthened his own position, and consequently that of his followers, that the laity have no say in church government or administration. Included among his sources was the solemn condemnation by the I Lateran Council (1123) of the practice of lay ap-

[14] Cf. Ullmann, *Medieval Papalism,* p. 35.

[15] *Summa,* at C. XVI, *principium* (Thaner, p. 56).

[16] The *Summa Parisiensis* qualified the principle of the bishop's authority by: "... nisi concessione ipsius sit libera, vel aliqua privilegio, forte domini papae, exempta."—At C. XVI, q. 7, c. 1 (McLaughlin, p. 142).

propriation of the offerings of the faithful.[17] He ended his short treatment of the problem in Causa X with the dictum:

> Premissis auctoribus ecclesiae . . . tam ecclesiae quam oblationes et facultates earum a laicorum dispensatione probantur esse immunes.[18]

In a second and more lengthy attack on this abuse, Gratian also appealed to legislation of the Gregorian Reform.[19]

Earlier in the *Decretum,* bishops who distributed tithes to laymen were declared guilty of simony.[20] They were to appoint procurators from among the clergy to care for the administration of the offerings of the faithful.[21]

Gratian's early commentators repeated and re-emphasized his own condemnation of lay alienation of church funds. Stephen of Tournai, for example, considered the right to possess tithes a *jus spirituale,* one which was not subject to prescription.[22] The author of the *Summa Parisiensis* looked upon the practice of alienation of tithes as contrary to the divine law.[23]

During the period in which Gratian wrote, the practice of lay investiture was still prevalent enough to warrant his devoting several canons to the problem. He attacked the practice at every level, by quoting legislation which condemned lay investiture in connection with the conferment of both episcopal benefices and the lesser dignities, his gen-

[17] C. X, q. 1, c. 14, which is c. 14 of the council as found in Mansi, XXI, 285. See Thomas, *Le droit de propriété,* pp. 67-68.

[18] At C. X, q. 1, c. 15; also: "Oblationes ecclesiae laicis usurpare non licet."—C. X, q. 1, c. 13 (rubric).

[19] E.g., at C. XVI, q. 7, c. 1, which is c. 6 of the Roman Council of 1078 as found in Mansi, XX, 510: "Decimas . . . possideri a laicis apostolica auctoritate prohibemus. . ."; cf. c. 3 of this Question, a summary of canons 1 and 6 of the council; D. I, *de cons.,* c. 10.

[20] "Symoniaci sunt episcopi qui decimas et oblationes laicis, non clericis distribuunt." —C. I, q. 3, c. 13 (rubrics).

[21] C. X, q. 1, cc. 21, 22.

[22] *Summa,* at C. XVI, q. 3 (Schulte, p. 226).

[23] "Omnis divinae legis et humanae auctoribus conclamat decimas a laicis nulla ratione debere possideri. Si secus fiat, certum est contra divina fieri mandata."—*Summa Paris.,* at C. XVI, q. 7 (McLaughlin, p. 186).

eral thesis being that no cleric could receive a church from a layman.[24] Several canons he recorded pronounced excommunication upon those guilty of conferring or accepting benefices by means of lay investiture.[25]

The rights of bishops in matters of investiture were also defended by the early Decretists. The teaching of Rufinus serves to illustrate this.

> . . . in hac questione asseritur usque ad sanguinem defendere debemus, scilicet quod per manum laicorum nec abbati nec alicui liceat accipere ecclesiam.[26]

Article 3. The Contribution of Gratian and the Early Canonists to the Development of the Right of Patronage

The greatest single contribution of Gratian and the twelfth century canonists to bring an end to the abuses of the proprietary system was the part they played in the development of the institute known as the *jus patronatus.* For it was this which proved to be the Church's ultimate weapon with which to end lay control over the smaller churches. Conditions in the twelfth century were conducive to a full development of such an institute. The lay lords had become less interested in their proprietary churches. The Church's incessant legislation to curb lay abuse of her authority had begun to have its effect. The *dominium* of the lay lord had become so restricted in its scope as to be a *proprietas inutilis.*[27] The comprehensive Germanic right of

[24] "Nullus clericus per laicos ecclesiasm obtineat."—C. XVI, q. 7, c. 20 (rubric); De manu laici episcopatus vel abbatia suscipi non debet."—C. XVI, q. 7, c. 12; cf. Marschesi, "De rationibus quae intercedunt inter Ecclesiam et res publicas in Gratiani Decreto," *Studia Gratiana post octava Decreti saecularia* (eds. J. Forchielli, A. Stickler, Bononiae, 1953-), III (1955), 186.

[25] E.g., at C. XVI, q. 7, cc. 16-19, from letters of Pope Paschal II (1099-1118), as found in Mansi, XX, 1072 (fragmentum); Jaffe, nn. 6609-6610.

[26] *Summa,* at C. XVI, q. 7, *principium* (Singer, p. 368).

[27] Cf. Thomas, *Le droit de propriété,* p. 105.

proprietas had broken down, under the pressure of this legislation, and as a natural consequence of the feudal system, into a number of separable rights, the most important of which was the right to nominate a cleric to be the pastor of the church, the *jus praesentationis*.[28] And only a few years before Gratian wrote, a General Council had declared any layman claiming ownership or control of church goods or property guilty of sacrilege.[29]

In a very brief dictum, Gratian presented his own views regarding the rights of lay founders of churches. This dictum became the nucleus around which early Decretist teaching on the right of patronage would develop, and it serves as an appropriate starting point for an examination of the role the first canonists played in the transformation of this right into an important canonical institute.

> Hic autem distinguendum est, quid juris fundatoris ecclesiarum in eis habent, vel quid non? Habent jus providendi, et consulendi, et sacerdotum inveniendi, sed non habent jus vendendi, vel donandi, vel utendi tamquam propriis.[30]

These words of Gratian leave the lay founder no room to claim any *dominium* or strict ownership over churches or church property. In this the *Magister* typifies eleventh and twelfth century thinking on the proprietary system. In earlier centuries, the radical *dominium* of the layman over his proprietary church had been explicitly recognized at times by Church councils, and traces of this recognition can be found in the *Decretum* itself.[31] Gradually, however, a change of emphasis took place. The *jus proprietarium*

[28] For this tendency, see Feine, *Kirchliche Rechtgeschichte*, I, 324.

[29] C. 4 of the I Lateran Council (1123), as found in Mansi, XXI, 282.

[30] C. XVI, q. 7, c. 30 (dictum).

[31] E.g., "A dominio constructoris oratorium non est auferendum." —C. XVI, q. 7, c. 33, a rubric introducing c. 8 of the Roman Synod of 826, as found in Mansi, XIV, 1006; "Ille debet abbas institui, quem sua congregatio et possessionis dominus ordinari poposcerit."—C. XVIII, q. 2, c. 4 (rubric), the canon being part of a letter attributed to Pope Pelagius I (555-560); Jaffe, n. 987.

was no longer described in terms suggestive of ownership. As a consequence of the reform efforts of the eleventh and twelfth centuries, and the teaching of the first canonists, the opinion that the lay founder and his heirs were only the recipients of a favor on the part of the Church became universal in ecclesiastical writings. The lay lords were no longer looked upon as owners, but as patrons, privileged to care for the church, and rewarded for that care by being allowed to nominate its priest.[32]

Because of this development, canonists who wrote after Gratian would explain away the references in the *Decretum* to ownership and the proprietary right of the lay founder. One unknown Decretist, writing around 1170, explained Gratian's use of the word *dominium* in this way: "a dominio, id est a jure patronatus; improprie enim hic dominium dicitur."[33] A few scattered references to the lay lord's *dominium* can be found in thirteenth century writings, but eventually the substitution of the *jus patronatus* for the *jus proprietarium* became a total one.

The principal element of this substitute for lay *dominium* was the *jus praesentationis*, for Gratian the *jus sacerdotum inveniendi.* In Distinction LXIII, Gratian recognized the practice of the Church in centuries past to tolerate some participation by the emperors and the people in the election of candidates to certain ecclesiastical offices. For him this participation did not involve what we now know as juris-

[32] Thomas, *Le droit de propriété*, pp. 105-128, where an entire chapter is devoted to the history of this substitution of the *jus patronatus* for *dominium.*

[33] Schulte, *Die Summa magistri Rufini zum Decretum* (Giessen, 1892), at C. XVI, q. 7, c. 33; cited by Thomas, *op. cit.*, p. 113. The work of Schulte is actually composed of the *Summa Antiquitate et Tempore,* and the *Summa Conditio ecclesiastice religionis,* twelfth century works borrowing extensively from Rufinus. See Kuttner, *Repertorium der Kanonistik, Prodromus corporis glossarum,* I (Studi et testi, 71, Citta del Vaticano, 1937), pp. 132-133, 178-179. Rolandus Bandinelli: "quod non dominium, sed servitutem credimus appellandam..."—*Summa,* at C. XVI, q. 7, c. 33 (Thaner, p. 57); "A dominio, id est dispositione..."—*Glossa ordinaria* on the same canon.

diction, but was either a mere *postulatio* of a candidate, or a *consensus* to an election already taken place.[34] In his mention of the *jus sacerdotum inveniendi,* however, Gratian was referring to still another early practice, the one which in the sixth and seventh centuries enabled the Church in Visigothic Spain to gain some control over the administration of the proprietary churches. This was the practice of allowing the lay founder of a church to present a candidate to the bishop for confirmation as its pastor. The efforts of the early canonists would be largely responsible for the triumphant return of this concession to fill the vacuum created by the lay founder's loss of the *jus proprietatis.*

Gratian's principal reference to the *jus praesentationis* was the rubric: "Fundatores ecclesiae ordinandos in ea episcopo offerant," introducing a canon of the IX Council of Toledo (655) which mentioned the lay founder as possessor of this right.[35] Coupled with this privilege of nominating the pastor was a corresponding obligation of the patron to care for the church. This too was referred to as a right, the *jus providendi.* Also, the lay lord was entitled to receive help from the temporal goods of the church when he was in extreme need, a right also recognized by the early Spanish councils.[36]

This brief attention given to the right of patronage by

[34] Regarding the role of the emperors in ecclesiastical elections, Gratian remarked: "Sed aliud est postulari, aliud eligi."—D. LXI, c. 11 (dictum). See Marschesi, "De rationisbus quae intercedunt Ecclesiam et res publicas in Gratiani Decreto," p. 190. The function of laymen at elections in the past was only to give humble assent to the choice made by the clergy. "Sed quod populis jubetur electioni interesse, non praecipitur advocari ad electionem faciendam, sed ad consensum electioni adhibendum. Sacerdotum enim... est electio, et fidelis populi est humiliter consentire."—D. LXIII, c. 25 (dictum); cf. D. LXIII, cc. 1, 10.

[35] C. XVI, q. 7, c. 32, which is c. 2 of the council as found in Bruns, I, 292. Cf. Stutz, "The Proprietary Church," p. 45.

[36] "Si vero fundatores ecclesiarum ad inopiam vergere ceperint, ab eisdem temporalis vitae suffragia percipiant."—C. XVI, q. 7, c. 30 (dictum); c. 8 of the IV Council of Toledo (633), as found in Bruns, I, 234.

Gratian brought considerable comment from the early Decretists. They began at once to analyze the nature of this right, and in so doing made important contributions to the development of the institute. Among these was the classification of the *jus patronatus* as a spiritual right, or as a right so connected with the spiritual that simony was involved in any attempt to sell it.

It seems to have been Rufinus who began the canonical development on this point. Like Gratian, he considered the *jus patronatus* to be composed of two principal rights, the right to provide for the church, and the right to nominate the clergy and present them to the bishop for investiture.

> Consistit autem hoc jus maxime in duobus, scilicet in provisione et sacerdotis vel prelati electione. In provisione ut, scilicet patronus ecclesiae diligenter provideat, ne res ecclesiae negligantur et pereant.... In sacerdotis electione, quia habet potestatem inveniendi et eligendi sacerdotum et offerendi episcopo, quatenus ipse episcopus eum in ecclesia statuat....[37]

Here the word *patronus* appears for the first time in Decretist writing to describe the lay founder.[38]

To give the precise nature of this right, Rufinus made a distinction which was in keeping with the concepts of clergy and laity found in the *Decretum*. He divided ecclesiastical rights into corporal rights, which could be possessed by a layman, and spiritual, which could be had only by ecclesiastical persons. Each of these rights, however, could be found attached to the other. The *jus patronatus*, he

[37] *Summa*, at C. XVI, q. 7, c. 26 (Singer, p. 368). Of the Decretists before Rufinus, Paucapalea looked upon the *jus patronatus* as an exception to the laws against lay investiture, a practice forbidden "nisi consensu apostolici vel episcopi fundatores ipsi pro sacro officio alicui presbytero ecclesiam illam commendare voluerint."—at C. XVI, q. 7, c. 12. Rolandus Bandinelli only noted that there was no right of government left to the lay founder but the *facultas eligendi.*—*Summa*, at C. XVI, q. 7, c. 33 (Thaner, p. 57).

[38] Stutz, "Gratian und die Eigenkirchen," p. 35; Kurtscheid, *Historia juris canonici*, p. 283.

believed, was such a mixture; it was a *jus corporale spirituali admixtum.*[39]

While Rufinus did not break completely with the concept of the lay lord as the *dominus possessionis,* it was but a small step from these distinctions to the conclusion that the right of patronage was primarily a spiritual one. About 1160, reference to the right of patronage as a *jus spirituale* is found in the *Summa Parisiensis.*[40] However, it is difficult to be certain whether or not this appearance was the result of direct speculation on the teaching of Rufinus. On the basis of McLaughlin's recent studies on the sources used by the author of the *Summa Parisiensis,* it seems to the writer that this was not the case.[41]

By 1160 or shortly thereafter, then, the *jus patronatus* had been described in canonical writing both as a spiritual right and as a temporal right connected with the spiritual. The canonists who wrote after this time would never come to perfect agreement as to which element was the more fundamental, the spiritual or the temporal. After 1234, however, the expression *jus spirituali annexum* was commonly used to describe the right. The reason for this was that St. Raymond of Peñafort added this expression to a decretal of Pope Alexander III appearing in the official

[39] "Sciendum est quod jus ecclesiasticum aliud corporale, aliud spirituale; corporale est quod potest competere etiam laicis, ut possessionum; spirituale est quod nunquam potest competere nisi ecclesiasticis personis, ut decimarum, oblationum. Jus autem corporale aliud nudum, aliud spirituali admixtum—ut patronatus—similiter spirituale aliud excisum, aliud corporali admixtum. Nudum, ut ecclesias consecrandi, missas cantandi, et huiusmodi; mixtum, ut jus ecclesiasticarum amministrationum." *Summa,* at C. XVI, q. 7, c. 26 (Singer, p. 370).

[40] "Quaeritur de jure repraesentandi utrum sit spirituale vel patrimoniale.... Jus autem spirituale istud est, non patrimoniale, quoniam non potest vendere, quod si venderit simoniam committit."—*Summa Paris.,* at C. XVI, q. 7, c. 26 (McLaughlin, p. 187).

[41] In the Introduction to his edition of the *Summa,* McLaughlin gives several arguments to support his view that the work was not dependent upon Rufinus. See the *Summa Paris.,* pp. xxvii-xxviii.

Decretals of Gregory IX.[42]

The description of the *jus patronatus* as a spiritual or quasi-spiritual right placed the canonists in a better position theoretically to meet the challenge of the lay lords. Stutz gives this summary of the importance of the spiritualization of the old right of *proprietas*:

> Where proprietary church law had been characterized by the subordination of the spiritual and public elements . . . to the one purely temporal element of ownership, patronage could be and was, defined as a jus temporale spirituali adnexum. The implication of this definition was twofold: in the first place, the interests and welfare of the church were of primary consideration . . . and secondly, this right was subject to ecclesiastical control and appertained henceforth, in case of controversy, to the jurisdiction of the church courts. Finally . . . patronage depended utterly on the goodwill and recognition of the Church. In this way the Church secured for itself the possibility, as time passed, of becoming . . . less accommodating; it could simply allow to fall into disuse those of the powers of patronage which no longer suited it. And this is precisely what occurred. Slowly and without upheaval the most valuable rights of patrons were reduced or brought to an end, until finally, after centuries of slow decline, nothing more remained than the modern canon law of patronage. . . .[43]

[42] ". . . quum inconveniens sit . . . vendi jus patronatus, quod est spirituali annexum . . ."—X, III, 38, c. 16; Jaffe, n. 13798. See Friedbegs's note here. Innocent IV: "Jus patronatus est jus quoddam, quod, neque mere temporale est neque mere spirituale . . ."—*Commentaria*, at X, III, 38, c. 1; Hostiensis: ". . . jus patronatus quodammodo ecclesiastici juris est, non tamen puri, sed mixti: quia quaedam temporalitas versatur, unde cadit in laicum et ideo nec omnino dicitur ecclesiasticum, sive spirituale, sed spirituali annexum."—*Commentaria*, at X, III, 38, c. 17, s.v. *ecclesiastici juris;* Panormitanus: ". . . sicut simonia committitur in mere spirituali, ita in annexo. . . . Nam jus patronatus est partim spirituale et partim temporale."—*Commentaria*, at X, III, 38, c. 16.

[43] "The Proprietary Church," pp. 69-70. Can. 1450, § 1: "Nullum patronatus jus ullo titulo constitui in posterum valide potest."

It involves no exaggeration to say that ecclesiastical patronage came both to life and to practical maturity in the forty years after the appearance of the *Decretum;* for these years saw not only the theoretic development of the *jus patronatus,* but an extensive application of the canonistic theories to practical cases as well. The solution of individual cases and problems by the ecclesiastical authorities in turn invited the canonists to additional speculation, with the result that even the minor characteristics of the institute had taken their final medieval form before 1180.

Credit for the success of the *jus patronatus* as a practical substitute for the old proprietary right must be given in large measure to the first of the great canonist popes, Alexander III. During his pontificate (1159-1181), Alexander issued a number of decretal letters solving problems which had arisen, especially in England, in regard to the exercise of the right of patronage. While a detailed examination of these responses and judicial decisions would be beyond the scope of this study, it will not be out of place to present here a few statistics which illustrate the importance of Alexander's efforts.

A number of Alexander's letters concerning the *jus patronatus* were incorporated in the decretal collections which appeared in the 1180's. For example, of the twenty-six *capitula* on patronage in the collection known as the *Appendix Concilii Lateranensis* (1181-1185), twenty-five are from the letters of Alexander.[44] Bernard of Pavia used decretals of Alexander for twenty-three of his thirty *capitula* on the subject of patronage in his *Breviarium extravagantium* (1181-1192), later known as the *Compilatio Prima.*[45] Finally, most of these *capitula* found in the *Compilatio Prima* were incorporated by St. Raymond of Peñafort in the official collection, the Decretals of Gregory IX, promulgated

[44] The collection is given in Mansi, XXII, 248-454; cols. 336-353 for the chapters on patronage. Cf. Stickler, *Historia,* pp. 221-225 for a description of these early collections.

[45] *Comp. I.,* III, 33, *de jure patronatus et ecclesiis a laicis concessis;* see Friedberg, *Quinque compilationes antiquae,* p. xviii (table).

in 1234.[46] The teaching of Pope Alexander III in this way became the very heart of the medieval doctrine of patronage.

* * * * *

This brief presentation of the canonists' first encounter with a body of laymen serves to illustrate the fact that Gratian and his disciples took a firm stand against lay interference of any kind in the Church's exercise of her authority. This position was to color every aspect of later canonical teaching on the status of laymen. For the legislation and opinion used by Gratian and the early Decretists to meet the challenge of the proprietary system would be cited time and again by the canonists of the thirteenth and fourteenth centuries. The attack of the canonists upon the proprietary church system, necessary though it was, can be held responsible, to a great extent, for the creation of the negative atmosphere which surrounded medieval canonistic theory regarding the layman's place in the life of the Church.

[46] X, III, 38, twenty-five chapters of which are from the letters of Alexander. For an example of how Alexander's decretals stimulated canonical thought, see the excerpts of the *Summa quaestionum* of the English Decretalist Honorius, written before 1190, given by S. Kuttner and E. Rathbone, "Anglo-Norman Canonists of the Twelfth Century," *Traditio,* VII (1949-1951), pp. 345-346. Making extensive use of the decretals of Alexander as his authority, Honorius devoted a dozen small *quaestiones* of D. 2, tit. 15 of his *Summa* to a variety of problems of patronage.

CHAPTER IV

THE NEGATIVE ATTITUDE OF THE MEDIEVAL CANONISTS TOWARD THE LAYMAN

The appearance in our century of the Catholic Action and Lay Apostolate movements has stimulated both speculative and historical study of the clergy-laity relationship as it has existed through the centuries. A common enough tendency among modern writers has been to place upon the Canon Law not a small share of responsibility for the belated arrival of the Age of the Layman; and the canonists of the High Middle Ages have not escaped criticism for giving the layman a very passive role in the life of the Church.[1]

It is this last point which has prompted the writer to examine in some detail the negative character of medieval canonistic writings in reference to the laity. This chapter is not intended as a defense of these recent assertions. Neither does it pretend to be an apology for the medieval canonists. Its purpose is only to show briefly by a few select illustrations just how negative the canonists' attitude toward the layman actually was, and to offer a few explanations for this phenomenon.

At the outset it must be admitted that the medieval canonists devoted only a small part of their discussions to the layman. When they did turn their attention to him, it was generally for the purpose of condemning his excesses, or of noting his subordinate role in ecclesiastical affairs in relation to the clergy. The type of legislation examined in

[1] For a discussion of this tendency among recent authors, see Philips, *The Role of the Laity in the Church* (trans. J. Gilbert and J. Moudry, Chicago: Fides Publishers, 1957), pp. 10-11, 16; Congar, *Lay People in the Church*, pp. xxviii-xxxi, pp. 13-15, and the authors there cited.

the preceding chapter continued to have a place in canonical writing long after Gratian and the first Decretists had made their attack on lay control of church property. In their commentary of this legislation, the Decretalists time and again cited the negative phraseology of the *Decretum.*

Perhaps the easiest way to see at a glance how negative this treatment of the layman was, is to examine the index to any of the sixteenth century printed editions of the medieval canonical works. For there, under the entry *laicus,* one usually finds only a list of the various offices, functions, and privileges denied the layman. Rarely will anything be found by way of constructive comment on his dignity as a member of the Church, or on his participation in her Sacramental life. And any comparison of this entry, as to size, with that under the word *clericus* in the same index will reveal at once how the canon law was primarily a law for the clergy. The following is typical:

> Laici de rebus ecclesiae nihil possunt disponere... Laici in ecclesia collegiata eligere non potest... Laici spiritualia sine periculo animae non possunt possidere... Laici in spiritualibus arbiter esse nequit... Laici patronus praesentando indignum, jus eligendi non perdit, nisi in casibus, in quibus eligens, vel collator perderet... Laici, an possint quandoque clericos capere... Laici quod nullam de rebus ecclesiasticiis administrationem habere debeant... Laici, an et quando clericos accusare, et contra eos testimonium fere possint.[2]

Another indication that the canonists made little mention of the layman's status other than to deny him any share of ecclesiastical authority is the persistent recurrence of certain stereotyped expressions in their writings. The most prominent of these was the statement that laymen enjoyed *nulla facultas de rebus ecclesiasticis.* In making use of it in their argumentation, the canonists were only repeating an expression which could be found both in official legislation, and in the *Decretum* of their master, Gratian. The

[2] Index to *Glossa ordinaria* on the *Decretales D. Gregorii Papae IX* (Romae, 1582), s.v. *Laicus.*

I Lateran Council (1123) had solemnly declared of laymen in regard to alienation of church property:

> ...juxta beatissimi Stephani papae sanctionem, statuimus, ut laici, quamvis religiosi sint, nullam tamen de ecclesiasticis rebus aliquid disponendi habeant facultatem.[3]

Gratian used the expression *nulla facultas* to condemn abuse of the Church's temporal goods by laymen.

> De rebus ecclesiasticis disponendi laicis nulla facultas relinquitur.[4]

The principle of *nulla facultas* entered the official Decretals of Gregory IX with the incorporation there of a letter of Pope Innocent III, which reads in part:

> Nos attendentes, quod laicis, etiam religiosis, super ecclesiis et personis ecclesiasticis nulla sit attributa facultas quos obsequendi manet necessitas, non auctoritas imperandi....[5]

What had originally only condemned the alienation of church property by laymen had by this time become a general slogan which the Decretalists would not hesitate to cite

[3] C. 4, as found in Mansi, XXI, 282. The source of this canon is a Pseudo-Isidorian decretal (*Ep. Stephani Secunda,* c. 12; Hinschius, *Decretales Pseudo-Isidorianae,* p. 186), in which the word *facultas* appears with two meanings: "...nullo tamen de eccesiasticis facultatibus aliquid disponendi legitur umquam attributa facultas." The material resources of the Church were frequently called the *facultates ecclesiae* in earlier centuries. See for example, c. 26 of the Council of Chalcedon (451) as found in Mansi, VII, 380 (*versio Dionesiana;* cf. C. XVI, q. 7, c. 21, and D. LXXIX, c. 4). The II Lateran Council (1139) decreed: "...nullam tamen habent disponendi de ecclesiasticis facultatibus potestatem."—c. 25; Mansi, XXI, 532. See also C. X, q. 1, c. 15 (dictum).

[4] D. XCVI, c. 1 (dictum), which introduced the proceedings of a Synod of Rome (502?) held by Pope Symmachus (Mansi, VIII, 265), as it appears in Pseudo-Isidore (*Decreta Symmachi Papae,* in Hinschius, *op. cit.,* p. 660).

[5] X, I, 2, c. 10; Potthast, n. 879. The IV Lateran Council's decree in 1215 against alienation (c. 44; Mansi, XXII, 1027-1028), which read: "laicis...nulla sit attributa potestas," is found at X, III, 13, c. 12.

when discussing clergy-laity relations involving ecclesiastical authority.[6]

Medieval canonical writing on the layman was also colored by a variety of negative definitions and descriptions of his status and of his conduct. How Gratian defined the layman by comparing his duties in life with those of the clergy has already been noted.[7] The tendency of his followers to do the same continued throughout the Middle Ages, and, in fact, has remained to the present day.[8]

Among the descriptions of laymen appearing in the writings under study, two of Hostiensis can be cited as typical of the period.

> ... plerumque tamen sunt crudeles laici, et tam terribiles, quod ecclesia non audet mutire (i?) ... et nobis oppido sunt infesti.[9]
>
> ... laici nobis oppido sunt infesti ... et mille modos habent defraudandi nos et subtrahendi ecclesiae....[10]

The statement here by Hostiensis that laymen are very

[6] Among other expressions the Decretalists could take from earlier canonists can be mentioned: "Laicus in Ecclesia aliquid statuendi facultatem non habet,"—C. XVI, q. 7, c. 23 (rubric); Rufinus: "... nulli laico non solum de ordinibus sed nec de aliquibus rebus ecclesiasticis disponendis nulla sit attributa licentia vel potestas..." —*Summa*, at D. XCVI, c. 1 (Singer, p. 191); Stephen of Tournai: "laicorum non est de ecclesiasticis negotiis constituere, vel definire..." —*Summa*, at D. XCVI, c. 1 (Schulte, p. 117); "Decernimus, ut laici ecclesiastica tractare negotia non praesumant..."—X, II, 1, c. 2 (Council of Rheims, 1148, c. 5; Mansi, XXI, 715).

[7] Above, p. 43?.

[8] This seems to be a natural occupational hazard of the canonist. Vermeersch-Creusen, for example, define laymen in this way: "sunt quibus omnis participatio potestatis sive jurisdictionis, sive praesertim ordinis deest."—*Epitome juris canonici*, I, n. 231; cf. Canon 118 of the Code of Canon Law.

[9] *Commentaria*, at X, III, 30, c. 17.

[10] *Commentaria*, at X, V, 3, c. 44. Also, Henricus de Bohic: "laici magis consueverint gravare ecclesiam quam clerici vel religiosi"—*Commentaria*, at X, V, 3, c. 44; and "... clerici magis sunt subditi et obedientes ad invicem, quam laici clericis..." *Commentaria*, at X, V, 3, c. 44. Cf. Panormitanus, *Commentaria*, at this decretal.

hostile to the clergy (*laici sunt nobis oppido infesti*) is deserving of special attention. This remark occurs repeatedly in the canonical literature of the thirteenth and fourteenth centuries, undoubtedly because of its use by Gratian himself. In Causa II of the *Decretum,* laymen are forbidden to bring judicial accusations against bishops for the following reason:

> ...quia non sunt eiusdem conversationis, et oppido eis quidam existunt infesti.[11]

The most famous use of this expression, however, occurs in the celebrated bull *Clericis laicos* of Pope Boniface VIII. This constitution, issued in 1296, was aimed at bringing to an end the growing practice of lay taxation of church property in France and England, as well as violations of personal clerical immunity from trial by the secular courts. It opened by declaring the tradition that laymen were inimical to the clergy still to be a valid one.

> Clericis laicos infestos oppido tradit antiquitas, quod et presentium experimenta temporum manieste declarant, dum suis finibus non contenti nituntur in vetitum, ad illicita frena relaxant nec prudenter attendunt quod sit eis in clericos ecclesiasticasve personas et bona interdicta potestas, ecclesiarum prelatis ecclesiis ecclesiasticisque personis regularibus et secularibus imponunt onera gravia....[12]

It is clear from the contexts in which these and similar expressions appear, that the complaints of the canonists were directed, for the most part, against the ruling classes of laymen. This segment of the faithful was the usual source from which sprang the abuses the canonists were vowed to eliminate. There is little if anything in the writ-

[11] C. II, q. 7, c. 5, from a Pseudo-Isidorian letter (*Eusebius ad Episcopos Galliae,* I, as found in Hinschius, *Decretales Pseudo-Isidorianae,* p. 230; Jaffe, n. 163). See also c. 14 of this Question, where c. 5 is paraphrased.

[12] VI°, III, 23, c. 3; Potthast, n. 24291. "It was a mournful epoch when a pope himself could declare in a solemn bull that from early times, and then more than ever, laymen were hostile towards the clergy."—Congar, *op. cit.,* p. 33, note 17.

ing of the canonists to indicate that the average layman was looked down upon, or considered hostile, merely on the strength of his not being a cleric. Were such the case, it would certainly have been an anomaly to find laymen admitted to the canon law schools of the medieval universities. As a matter of fact, however, a number of laymen are listed among the influential canonists of the late twelfth and the thirteenth centuries, among them the author of the *Glossa ordinaria* to Boniface VIII's *Liber Sextus,* Joannes Andreae.[13]

The modern student of the Lay Apostolate can rightfully be disappointed to discover that the medieval canonists were not more constructive in their teaching on the status of the layman. And yet the attitude of these men, however unfortunate, is understandable. The nature of the Canon Law itself is such as to preclude from its framework an extensive, positive treatment of the layman's everyday Catholic life. By far the majority of its canons are concerned with the well organized conduct of ecclesiastical affairs by the hierarchy, and particularly with the correct administration of the Sacraments by the Church's appointed ministers. Regarding this, Congar observes:

> . . . indeed the Code is not the place to look for an adequate answer to questions about the laity. In its origins, history and very nature canon law is principally a systematising of sacramental *cultus,* and it is normal that it should be chiefly a code for clerics and sacred matters.[14]

[13] "The lay element was almost entirely absent in the twelfth century; it slowly emerged in the thirteenth century and was firmly established in the fourteenth, especially after it was possible to graduate in both the civil and canon laws. Egidius Fuscararius, Dynus de Muxellano and Martinus de Fano may be taken as outstanding lay examples of the thirteenth century, . . . Joannes Andreae, . . . Petrus de Ancharano, Johannes de Lignano, Antonius de Butrio, Johannes ab Imola—these were only a few of the better known personalities." —Ullman, *Medieval Papalism,* p. 6.

[14] *Lay People in the Church,* p. xxx. For a recent attempt to give a more positive treatment of the layman's rights and duties as found in ecclesiastical law, see the work of March, *Derechos y Deberes de*

The way in which the medieval Canon Law developed was not conducive to a more positive approach toward the layman on the part of the canonists. It was a science which was formed by commentary on authoritative writing. Whether the authority involved was scholastic, or ecclesiastical, or a combination of both, the Decretists and Decretalists quite naturally would look to their authoritative sources for the subject matter of their discussions, and for the arguments with which to support their conclusions.

Had Gratian devoted any of his *dicta* to an examination of the layman's role as cooperator with the hierarchy in the spread of the Faith, it is reasonable to assume that the canonists would have followed his example, and would even have elaborated considerably upon his remarks. As it happened, Gratian's only treatise on the layman consisted of a justified attack upon lay control of churches and ecclesiastical appointments. How this was partly responsible for the negative atmosphere surrounding all medieval canonical writing has been considered in the previous chapter. One colorful example can be added here, however, to illustrate how Gratian provided the canonists with arguments for their defense of the Church's rights, and at the same time unwittingly placed an obstacle in the way of their taking a constructive attitude toward the layman in their writings. There is recorded in the *Decretum* a canon of the Second Synod of Seville (619) forbidding bishops to appoint laymen as procurators of ecclesiastical goods. The Synod's reasons given for this prohibition are these:

> Indecorum est enim laicum vicarium episcopi esse et viros ecclesiasticos judicare. In uno enim eodemque officio non debet dispar esse professio. Quod etiam in lege divina prohibetur, dicente Moyse: "Non arabis in bove simul et asino," id est: homines diversae professionis in uno officio simul non sociabis.[15]

los Seglares en la Vida Social de la Iglesia (Barcelona: Herder, 1954).

[15] C. XVI, q. 7, c. 22, which is c. 9 of the Synod as given by Bruns, II. 72; cf. Deuteronomy, 22, 10.

There is nothing in a text such as this which would prompt a Decretist to comment on the need for lay cooperation with the hierarchy.[16]

Neither did the decretal legislation of the late twelfth and thirteenth centuries favor the development of positive discussions by the canonists of the layman's place in the Church. Many of the problems of lay abuse remained from Gratian's day, and this, coupled with the opening of new areas of conflict between lay rulers and Church authorities, invited additional legislation as negative in character as that found in the *Decretum*.[17] Moreover, the rise of the medieval heresies in the second half of the twelfth century brought with it serious challenges to the authority of the Church by laymen.

The development of the provisions of the medieval Canon Law to counteract the practice of lay preaching by members of these heretical sects can be traced briefly here as being typical of the manner in which legislation so negative in its orientation found its way into the official decretal collections. It was the Waldensian heresy in particular which provoked the Church in the twelfth century to condemn preaching by laymen. The founder of this sect, Peter Waldo, had vowed to preach to all the virtue of poverty.

[16] Joannes Teutonicus: "Et hoc probat tribus rationibus. Prima est quia in uno et eodem officio non debet esse dispar professio. Secunda est, quia lex Mosaica dicit, Non arabis in bove et asino. Tertia est, quia convenire non possunt, quibus vota et studia sunt diversa." —*Glossa ordinaria*, on C. XVI, q. 7, c. 22. (In another place, Joannes gave as his opinion that bishops could make temporary appointments of lay procurators. See *Glossa ordinaria*, on D. XCVI, c. 1, s.v. *praeter Romanam Pontificem*.) Guido de Baysio: "in bove, id est, fatuos sapientibus."—Rosarium, at C. XVI, q. 7, c. 22, s.v. *in bove*.

[17] As examples of legislation to end lay alienation and taxation of church property, see X, III, 13; X, III, 30; X, III, 49, c. 4; VI°, II, 9; VI°, III, 23. A number of decretals were concerned with questions of clerical immunity from the secular courts; for example, at X, II, 1; X, II, 2; VI°, II, 2; VI°, III, 23, c. 4. Cf. Downs, *The Concept of Clerical Immunity*, The Catholic University of America Canon Law Studies, n. 126 (Washington, D.C.: The Catholic University of America Press, 1941), pp. 21-28.

When the Archbishop of Lyons forbade the group to preach, they appealed, in 1179, to Pope Alexander III, who approved of their life of poverty, but did not overrule the Archbishop's prohibition.[18] As early as 1184, Pope Lucius III issued a strong condemnation of the Waldensian preaching.[19] The decree was cited almost verbatim by the IV Lateran Council (1215), and in turn was incorporated in the official Decretals of Pope Gregory IX.[20]

In addition to this general decree against unauthorized preaching, the Decretals of Gregory IX contained excerpts from two papal letters on the subject. One of these was originally directed to the people of the diocese of Metz by Pope Innocent III in 1199. A group of lay men and women there had been reported as giving discourses on the Scriptures among themselves. Pope Innocent praised their desire to learn more about the Scriptures, but censured them for usurping the preaching office.

> Licet autem desiderium intelligendi divinas scripturas, et secundum eas studium adhortandi, reprehendendum non sit, sed potius commendandum; in eo tamen apparent quidam laici merito arguendi . . . officium praedicationis Christi sibi usurpant . . . Quum igitur doctorum ordo sit quasi praecipuus in ecclesia, non debet sibi quisquam indifferenter praedicationis officium usurpare. . . .[21]

The second decretal, from a letter of Pope Gregory IX to

[18] Hughes, *A History of the Church,* II, 336.

[19] Mansi, XXII, 477.

[20] "Quia vero nonnulli sub specie pietatis virtutem eius, juxta quod sit Apostolus abnegantes, auctoritatem sibi vendicant praedicandi . . . omnes, qui prohibiti vel non missi, praeter auctoritatem ab Apostolica Sede vel catholico episcopo loci susceptam, publicae vel privatim praedicationis officium usurpare praesumpserint, excommunicationis vinculo innodentur . . ."—c. 3; Mansi, XXI, 990; X, V, 7, c. 13. The juridic foundation of our modern teaching on the necessity of a canonical *missio* in order to preach is contained here. Cf. Can. 1328, and Sigur, "Lay Cooperation with the Magisterium," *The Jurist,* XIII (1953), 274-280.

[21] X, V, 7, c. 12; Potthast, n. 780. Sigur (*op. cit.,* p. 272) mistakenly attributes this letter to Gregory IX.

the Archbishop of Milan, contained a similar prohibition.[22] Finally, a decretal letter of Pope Alexander IV forbidding lay disputations on matters of Faith was given a place in the *Liber Sextus* of Pope Boniface VIII.[23]

The negative attitude toward the layman which legislation such as this helped to produce, was to remain a characteristic of medieval canonical writing in spite of the growth of speculation on the corporate structure of the Church. The High Middle Ages was a time of great progress in theoretical studies of the nature of corporate bodies, and the canonists devoted a considerable amount of effort to discussions on the relative rights of head and members of these societies.[24]

To give but one example, the canonists discussed and proposed a variety of theories as to where actual *dominium*

[22] "Nos, attendentes, quod doctorum ordo est in ecclesia Dei quasi praecipuus, mandamus, quatenus ... interdicas laicis universis, cuiuscunque ordinis censeantur, usurpare officium praedicandi."—X, V, 7, c. 14; Potthast, n. 9675.

[23] "Inhibemus quoque, ne cuiquam laicae personae liceat publice vel privatim de fide catholica disputare ..."—VI°, V, 2, c. 2; Potthast, n. 18115. The Decretalists could point to the *Decretum* to corroborate this stand. See D. XXIII, c. 29; C. XVI, q. 1, c. 19, and below, p. 88.

[24] See Tierney, *Conciliar Theory*, pp. 87-131, for a thorough treatment of Decretalist theories of the Church as a corporation. Among the reasons for the canonists taking up questions of corporation law, Dr. Tierney (p. 97) notes: "In spite of the persistent tendency towards papal centralization, the whole Church, no less than the secular states, remained in a sense a federation of semi-autonomous units, a union of innumerable greater or lesser corporate bodies. Bishoprics, abbeys and priories, colleges, chantries and guilds, religious orders, congregations and confraternities all ... exercised substantial rights of self-government. These lesser corporations had their constitutional problems no less than the all-embracing *universitas* of the whole Church.... Moreover, the growth of new forms of corporate life in the Church, especially the universities and the orders of friars with their intricate systems of representative government, both reflected the half-formed juristic ideas of the age and stimulated the canonists to clarify those ideas, and to apply them to other ecclesiastical communities."

over church property resided in the ecclesiastical corporation. Among the variety of answers they gave to the question, the *congregatio fidelium,* the *aggregatio fidelium,* and the *universitas loci* were described as holding this radical ownership.[25] In keeping with theories such as these, the bishop could be described as only the procurator of the ecclesiastical goods of all the faithful.[26] But there was never any doubt in the minds of the canonists as to who possessed the actual authority over these goods. So plentiful were their legal sources in this matter that, coroporation theories notwithstanding, they were never in any danger of compromising with the laity on a question as fundamental as control of church property.

[25] Thus Huguccio: "... illa bona competant ecclesiae catholicorum, non enim parietibus sed congregationi fidelium"—as cited by Tierney, *op. cit.,* p. 118; Innocent IV: "Non praelatus sed Christus dominium et possessionem rerum ecclesiae habet... vel ecclesiae habet possessionem et proprietatem... id est aggregatio fidelium quae est corpus Christi capitis."—*Commentaria,* at X, II, 12, c. 4; Guido de Baysio: "... Goffredus dicit verius est quod sunt universitatis illius loci..." —*Rosarium,* at C. XII, q. 1, c. 13. All these views are discussed by Tierney, *op. cit.,* pp. 117-127; 140-141.

[26] Hostiensis: "prelatus procurator est habens generalem et liberam administrationem."—*Commentaria,* at X, I, 36, c. 3. For Gratian and the early Decretists the notion of the bishop as procurator was chiefly metaphorical, but it took on a more formal juridic character as corporation ideas developed. See Tierney, *op. cit.,* p. 120 .

CHAPTER V

THE LAYMAN AND THE POSSESSION OF ECCLESIASTICAL JURISDICTION

A study of the possibility of laymen possessing ecclesiastical jurisdiction is today only of speculative interest, for Canon 118 of the Code of Canon Law limits the exercise of the power of jurisdiction to clerics.[1] However, since the medieval canonists so ardently proclaimed the principle that laymen were to have no authority in the government of the Church or in the management of her temporal affairs, it is of interest to examine their writings for possible exceptions to their general rule, particularly in relation to the power of jurisdiction.

The teaching of the medieval canonists regarding the possessor of jurisdiction offers subject matter for extensive research. A satisfactory understanding of this question cannot be had until the concepts of jurisdiction and administration had by the canonists are more carefully analyzed; and this in turn must await further studies on the complicated terminology and phraseology used by the canonists when writing of the powers of government. Rather than attempt to survey a field of study as large as this, the writer has chosen to explore in the present chapter two very specific areas where the canonists might be expected to concede jurisdictional authority to the layman.

ARTICLE 1. THE STATUS OF THE LAYMAN ELECTED POPE

In his address to the Second World Congress for the Lay Apostolate, the late Pope Pius XII noted that a layman, were he to be chosen Pope, would have from the moment

[1]"Soli clerici possunt potestatem sive ordinis sive jurisdictionis ecclesiasticae . . . obtinere."

of his acceptance of the election, and before his ordination, both the power to teach and to govern the Church, and the prerogative of infallibility.[2] This is an interesting application of the principles of Canon 219 of the Code of Canon Law, which declares that the Roman Pontiff, once legitimately elected, has from the moment of his acceptance of that election, by divine right, full power of supreme jurisdiction in the Church.[3]

In the unusual circumstances described by the Holy Father, a layman would have, for a time at least, supreme jurisdiction over the whole Church, and this by ordinary power. The present article examines the teaching of the medieval canonists on the juridic status of the Pope-elect, with a view toward discovering what authority they implicitly or explicitly attributed to a layman chosen to be Pope.

SECTION 1. DERETIST TEACHING ON THE AUTHORITY OF THE PAPA ELECTUS NON CONSECRATUS

The canonists took up the question of the status of the newly elected Pope only by degrees. It was for them a canonical problem of their own making; and a study of its gradual formulation illustrates how the science of Canon Law developed from one commentary on the *Decretum* to the next.

That laymen were generally forbidden to be elected Pope was well defined canonical doctrine when Gratian wrote. Among the more important legislation on papal elections to be found in the *Decretum* are excerpts from the Lateran

[2] "...si un laïc était élu Pape, il ne pourrait accepter l'élection qu'a condition d'être apte à recevoir l'ordination et disposé à se faire ordonner; le pouvoir d'enseigner et de gouverner, ainsi que le charisme de l'infaillibilité, lui seraient accordés dès l'instant de son acceptation, même avant son ordination..."—Address of Oct. 5, 1957, as given in the *Acta Apostolicae Sedis*, XXXXIX (1957), p. 924.

[3] "Romanus Pontifex, legitime electus, statim ab acceptata electione, obtinet, jure divino, plenam supremae jurisdictionis potestatem."

Synod held by Pope Stephen III in 769, in which it was decreed that, for the future, the Pope was to be chosen only from among the *cardinales presbyteri* or the deacons of Rome.[4]

Also in the *Decretum* was an electoral law that gave the Decretists an opportunity to theorize on the status of the Pope-elect before his consecration. This was the decree on papal elections promulgated by Pope Nicholas II in the Lateran Synod of 1059, which reserved the election of the Pope to the *cardinales episcopi* of Rome, aided by their *clerici cardinales*. Other members of the clergy, together with the people, were only to consent to the election.[5] One of the emergency provisions of this decree stated that the Pope-elect would have complete authority as Pope should conditions makes his formal enthronement (*inthronizatio*) impossible.

> Plane, postquam electio fuerit facta, si bellica tempestas vel qualiscumque hominium conatus malignatis studio restiterit, ut is, qui electus est, in apostolica sede juxta consuetudinem inthronizari non valeat, electus tamen, sicut vere Papa, auctoritatem obtineat regendi Romanam ecclesiasm, et disponendi omnes facultates illius; quod beatum

[4] "Oportebat, ut haec sacrosancta domina nostra Romana ecclesia... rite ordinaretur, et in apostolatus culmen unus de cardinalibus presbysteris aut diaconibus consecraretur."—D. LXXIX, c. 3, which is *actio* 3 of the Synod as found in Mansi, XII, 719; "Si quis ex episcopis, vel monachis, vel laicis... prorumpens in gradum filiorum sanctae Romanae ecclesiae, id est presbyterorum cardinalium et diaconorum ire presumpserit,... et ad summum pontificalem honorem ascendere voluerit, ipsi et sibi faventibus fiat perpetuum anathema..." —D. LXXIX, c. 5 (*actio* 4; Mansi, XII, 720); see also D. LXXIX, c. 4. For the tradition of Gratian's texts here, see Kuttner, "Cardinalis: The History of a Canonical Concept," *Traditio*, III (1945), p. 149, n. 24; and pp. 148-151, where this first reference to the *presbyteri cardinales* of the Roman Church is discussed.

[5] D. XXIII, c. 1; *MGH*, *Legum sectio IV*, *Constitutiones*, I (ed. L. Weiland, Hanoverae, 1893), 539-541; Mansi, XIX, 903-904. For the *clerici cardinales* as distinct from the rest of the Roman clergy, see Kuttner, "Cardinalis," pp. 146-152.

Gregorium ante consecrationem suam fecisse cognovimus.[6]

The early Decretists, in their commentary on this part of the election decree, first attempted to explain the degree of authority had by a bishop-elect before his consecration. It was here that Rufinus made his distinction between the bishop's *potestas administrationis,* and his *plenitudo auctoritatis,* the latter being acquired only by episcopal consecration.[7]

Rufinus did not take up the question of the need for confirmation of the bishop's election by the metropolitan. After him, however, canonical teaching on the necessity of such a confirmation developed rapidly. Along with this came comparisons of the status of a bishop-elect with that of the Pope-elect. Stephen of Tournai, writing in the 1160's, believed election of a bishop to be nothing more than *approbatio* of the candidate. He associated with *confirmatio* the authority which Rufinus believed came with election. The Roman Pontiff's election was for him an exception, since he had, prior to consecration, the *potestas regendi romanam ecclesiam.*[8] From this it can be seen that the statement

[6] D. XXIII, c. 1. Weiland's text (*op. cit.*, p. 540, n. 8) reads: "electus tamen, sicut Papa, auctoritatem obtineat. . . ." This provision appears again at D. LXXXIX, c. 9, from an altered text of the Roman Synod of 1060; Weiland, pp. 550-551; Mansi, XIX, 899. Cf. Kuttner, "Cardinalis," p. 174, n. 99, for the transmission of this text to Gratian.

[7] See above p. 16, n. 51.

[8] Hinc habes, quod electus papa ante consecrationem habet potestatem regendi romanam ecclesiam. . . .Nec est contrarium . . .quod episcopi se magis existiment ex electione approbatos. Et revera ex sola electione approbantur, ex confirmatione electionis etiam praemissam potestatem consequuntur. Confirmata enim electione possunt etiam divinum officium interdicere et a beneficio clericos ex justa causa suspendere, non tamen sine capituli sui auctoritate, ordines autem auferre alicui non potest. . . . Habet enim electus potestatem administrationis, nòn auctoritoritatem dignitatis."—*Summa,* at D. XXIII, c. 1 (Schulte, p. 35); see Benson, "From Election to Consecration: Studies on the Constitutional Status of an *Electus* in the High Middle Ages" (unpublished Ph.D. dissertation, Princeton University, 1957), pp. 75-76. The writer wishes to thank Dr. Benson and the Princeton University Li-

of Nicholas II concerning the Pope's *potestas regendi* in cases where his enthronement could not take place had been converted, by the 1160's, into a new general principle, valid for every papal election, to the effect that the Pope had this power to rule from the moment he was chosen by the cardinals.[9]

That the Pope's election had no need of any special confirmation was implied by Stephen of Tournai, inasmuch as he assigned to the Pope at the time of his election all the juridic effects of electoral confirmation. Earlier, Pope Nicholas in his decree had compared the function of the *cardinales episcopi* in papal elections to that of the metropolitan in the election of bishops.[10] These two lines of thought fused, and the Decretists soon were teaching that papal elections did involve some kind of *confirmatio,* for the new Pope was confirmed by the cardinals at the moment of his election. This view became explicit by the time of Simon of Bisignano (ca. 1177-1179). It was a principle which would be cited frequently by future canonists.[11]

brary for making this work available for his use. For the meaning of the expression *Romana ecclesia* to the Decretists, see Tierney, *Conciliar Theory,* p. 36.

[9] "In the papal election decree, the right to administer immediately after election was a special stipulation for extraordinary and unsettled conditions. A century later, Stephen of Tournai assumed that this right was automatically conferred by the papal election. In other words, between 1059 and the 1160's, the exceptional case had become the usual rule."—Benson, *op. cit.,* pp. 90-91.

[10] "Quia sedes apostolica cunctis in orbe terrarum prefertur ecclesiis atque ideo super se metropolitanum habere non potest, cardinales episcopi procul dubio metropolitani vice funguntur, qui videlicet electum antistitem ad apostolici culminis apicem provehunt."—D. XXIII, c. 1; Weiland, *op. cit.,* p. 540, n. 5.

[11] Simon of Bisignano: "Hinc collige, quod summus pontifex statim cum eligitur, potest res ecclesie amministrare, clericos suspendere et prebendas dare.... Et hoc ideo, quia ab eisdem eligitur et confirmatur."—*Summa,* at D. XXIII, c. 1, as quoted by Benson, *op. cit.,* Ch. I, note 78; Huguccio: Ipse enim eligitur confirmando et confirmatur eligendo..."—*Summa,* at D. LXXIX, c. 9, as quoted by Tierney, *op. cit.,* p. 144. Innocent III said of his union, as Pope, with the Church: "Illud autem conjugium, quod ego sponsus cum hoc sponsa

By the 1160's the canonists began to speculate on the precise nature of the authority possessed by a Pope-elect who was not a bishop. This development came at a time when the distinction between the power of orders and that of jurisdiction was becoming more clear to the canonists. The Decretists would quite naturally employ this distinction when discussing the *papa electus non consecratus.* The result of this speculation can be seen in Huguccio's declaration that the Pope, before his consecration as a bishop, possessed all the papal authority deriving from jurisdiction; not, however, that which depended upon ordination.

> Set ecce papa est electus et nondum est episcopus, potest deponere vel degradare clericos? Potest suspendere uel excommunicare? Utique, et ut generalem faciam doctrinam, omnia que sunt tantum jurisdictionis set non illa que sunt ordinis. Potest ergo deponere, degradare, excommunicare, suspendere, prebendas dare et auferre et huiusmodi, sed non potest clericos ordinare, crisma conficere, altaria uel ecclesias consecrare et huiusmodi. Prima enim potius sunt jurisdictionis quam ordinis, hec autem ex ordine proueniunt, nam insacratus uel inordinatus consecrare uel ordinare non potest. . . .[12]

This is as close as the Decretists would come to an explicit consideration of the status of the layman elected Pope. Huguccio's references to the ordination of clerics, the blessing of chrism, and the consecration of altars and churches indicate he was concerned only with the Pope-elect who was not a bishop, and did not consider the status of one who was not already a priest or at least a cleric. A Decretist of the early thirteenth century would, in fact, paraphrase Huguccio's distinction between jurisdiction and orders here as one between *jurisdictio* and *consecratio.*[13]

contraxi, simul fuit initiatum et ratum; quia Romanus pontifex cum eligitur, confirmatur, et cum confirmatur, eligitur."—*Sermones de diversis*, 3; *MPL*, CCXVII, 663.

[12] *Summa*, at D. XXIII, c. 1, s.v. *disponendi omnes facultates*, as quoted by Benson, *op. cit.*, Ch. I, note 92.

[13] *Summa Animal est substantia*: ". . . ex ipsa electione confirmatur

The importance of these fifty years of Decretist speculation on the election decree of Pope Nicholas II should not be underestimated. Though they did not explicitly treat of the authority which would be possessed by a layman elected Pope, the Decretists did provide the Canon Law with the distinction we now recognize as fundamental to any discussion of the problem, namely that existing between the powers of jurisdiction and orders. They applied this distinction to the case of a Pope-elect who was not a bishop, and in so doing implied that a layman would have the power of jurisdiction were he to be chosen Pope. For them the problem of the status of the new Pope before consecration was only an academic one. A century later the question would be taken up once again at the very point where Huguccio left off; and for more practical reasons which must now be seen, the layman elected Pope would have attributed to him explicitly the same authority Huguccio gave to the *papa non consecratus*.

SECTION 2. PUBLICIST TEACHING ON THE STATUS OF THE LAYMAN ELECTED POPE

The thirteenth century Decretalists occasionally made reference to the Decretist theories on the authority of the Pope-elect before consecration, especially during the period known as the Interregnum (1250-1312), which began with the death of the Emperor Frederick II. During these years students of both the canon and the civil law debated the question of the authority possessed by the Emperor-elect before his coronation in Rome. Among the canonists taking part in the discussions, Guilielmus Durantis made use of these earlier views on the status of the *papa electus* to reinforce his arguments in favor of the Emperor elect's

et statim habet potestatem et jus in omnibus illis que sunt jurisdictionis, que autem sunt consecrationis non habet antequam consecratus. Unde antequam sit consecratus non potest ordinem conferre . . ."—at D. XXIII, c. 1, s.v. *sicut*, as quoted by Benson, *op. cit.*, Ch. I, note 140. Kuttner (*Repertorium*, pp. 206-207) dates the *Summa* between 1206 and 1210.

possession of authority.[14] However, there is no evidence available to the writer which would indicate that the specific question of the layman elected Pope was ever expressly proposed for discussion by the Decretalists before the reign of Pope Boniface VIII began in 1294.[15]

The occasion for renewed interest in the status of the Pope-elect came at the turn of the century, with the violent struggle between Pope Boniface VIII and the Colonna faction of cardinals and nobles. Opposition to the Pope's policy of favoring his own family, the Gaetani, led the Colonna into open rebellion. Shortly after an attack upon a papal convoy by one of the Colonna in May of 1297, the two cardinals of the clan, James and Peter, issued a series of manifestoes in which they attacked the validity of Boniface's election. In the first of these, Boniface was declared to be a usurper of the papacy on the grounds that the resignation of his predecessor, Celestine V, could in no way be justified. The controversy which developed as a result of this charge became an international issue. The French King, Philip the Fair, used the debate over the lawfulness of the papal election to good advantage in his own encounter with the Pope, going so far as to put pressure on the University of Paris to declare the election of Boniface invalid.[16]

[14] "Nota ex sola Principium electione et ante confirmationem aliquam, verus est Imperator . . . et Papa ex sole electione consequitur plenam potestatem regendi, et cum non habet superiorem, cum eligitur, confirmatur . . ."—*Speculum juris*, Lib. II, tit. 2, n. 18 (p. 424), repeated by Guido de Baysio, *Rosarium*, at D. XXIII, c. 1, s.v. *facultates*. "Chiefly for practical reasons Durandus opined that the prince enjoyed full powers before his consecration because otherwise the donations to the Holy See made by Rudolf of Hapsburg would be invalid."—Kantorowicz, *The King's Two Bodies, A Study in Mediaeval Political Theology* (Princeton, N.J.: Princeton University Press, 1957), p. 325; also pp. 324-328 for details of this debate.

[15] The possibility of one or the other thirteenth-century canonist taking up the matter cannot, of course, be overlooked.

[16] For the Pope's war with the Colonna, and the repercussions of the Colonna attack on the validity of the papal election, see Boase, *Boniface VIII* (London: Constable and Co., 1933), pp. 159-185; Hughes, *A History of the Church*, III, pp. 51-69.

In their manifesto, the Colonna did not advert to the distinction between the powers of orders and of jurisdiction. Several of their theses, in fact, were based on a confused notion of the nature of episcopal orders. They argued, for example:

> Et nimis extraneum et a ratione remotum apparet, quod summus pontifex qui est . . . vicarius Jesu Christi, qui est sacerdos in aeternum, possit absolvi ab alio, quam ab ipso Deo, et quod quandiu vixerit non maneat summus pontifex. . . .[17]

The legitimate character of the Pope's election was vigorously defended by a small group of writers who are now known as the pro-papal publicists. To encounter the arguments of the Colonna, they quite naturally looked to Huguccio's distinction between orders and jurisdiction, by this time well established canonical doctrine, and particularly to his use of this distinction in regard to the Pope-elect not a bishop.[18]

In presenting this distinction, however, the publicists went beyond the speculation of the Decretists. Giles of Rome, writing shortly after the first Colonna manifesto in 1297, emphasized that if one not a priest were to be

[17] Manifesto of May 10, 1297; *Archiv für Literatur-und Kirchengeschichte*, V (1889), 512.

[18] Giles of Rome: "Sed dicemus, quod ille idem qui non est pontifex potest habere plenam jurisdictionem, et authoritatem summi Pontificis: ut si aliquis sit in Papam electus antequam ordinetur in Episcopum, habebit plenam jurisdictionem Summi Pontificis, non tamen erit Summus Pontifex nisi sit Pontifex."—*De renuntiatione papae*, Cap. X, in *Bibliotheca maxima pontificia* (ed. J. Thoma de Rocaberti, 21 vols., Romae, 1697-1699), II, p. 21; Augustinus Triumphus: "potestas papae distincta est ab omnibus quia solus ipse assumptus est in plenitudinem potestatis totius Ecclesiae: non tamen talis distinctio dicit alterius potestatis ordinis . . . quia nihil potest pape in potestate ordinis nisi quantum potest presbyter vel simplex episcopus."—*Summa de potestate ecclesiastica* (Augustae Vindelicorum, 1473), Q. IV, 1, fol. 46. The views of Augustinus on papal jurisdiction are summarized by Wilks, "Papa est Nomen Jurisdictionis: Augustinus Triumphus and the Papal Vicariate of Christ," *The Journal of Theological Studies*, N.S. VIII (1957), 71-91; 256-271.

elected Pope, he would nevertheless have all the authority that pertained to papal jurisdiction.

> Et exinde est quod electus in Papam; si non sit Sacerdos, omnem jurisdictionem habet quae potest pertinere ad Papam: sed nihil habet de his quae sunt ordinis Sacerdotalis, nec de his quae sunt ordinis episcopalis. . . .[19]

It was only a small step from this proposition to an explicit declaration that a layman elected Pope would have the same authority. This step was taken by 1320, when Augustinus Triumphus declared in his extremely pro-papal *Summa de potestate ecclesiastica*:

> Puto quod supposito quod esset laicus et non esset constitutus in sacris electus in papam esset verus papa, et haberet omnem potestatem jurisdictionis papalis. . . .[20]

Another important doctrine regarding the layman is found in the *Summa* of Augustinus. Emphasis on the distinction between orders and jurisdiction, which had become a characteristic of the publicist writing, led this publicist to conclude that laymen could be delegated by the Pope for any and all acts of ecclesiastical jurisdiction.

> Dicendum quod ad officium clericale vel potest pertinere potestas ordinis vel jurisdictionis potestas . . . Potestas vero jurisdictionis laico potest committi dummodo ad hoc idoneitatem habeat . . . unde ex commissione pape puto quod laicus po-

[19] *De renuntiatione papae*, Cap. X (Rocaberti, II, 31); cf. Cap. X, 4 (p. 26). The same year, the leader of the Franciscan Spirituals, Peter John Olivi, wrote in his reply to the Colonna: ". . . si aliquis nondum sacerdos sit in papam electus, eo ipso habet totam papalem jurisdictionem, et tamen non habet ordinem sacerdotalem nec episcopalem."—*De renuntiatione pape* (ed. P. L. Oliger), in *Archivum Franciscanum Historicum*, XI (1918), p. 357.

[20] Q. IV, 2, ad 1, fol. 48. In his earlier work (ca. 1308), Augustinus did not explicitly mention the layman in his example: "potest alicui convenire potestas jurisdictionis, cui non convenit potestas ordinis, ut si aliquis existens diaconus vel subdiaconus et fiat papa . . ."—*Tractatus brevis de duplici potestate prelatorum et laicorum*, in Scholz, *Die Publizistik zur Zeit Phillips des Schönen und Bonifaz' VIII* (Stuttgart: Verlag von F. Enke, 1903), p. 491.

> test excommunicare benefica ecclesiastica conferre et omnia quod ex jurisdictione perveniunt.[21]

The power of orders, concerned as it was with the Eucharist, the *corpus Christi verum,* could not be so delegated. But jurisdiction he believed could be entrusted to the layman, because it involved authority over the Church, the *corpus Christi mysticum,* which was composed of both clergy and laity.[22]

Among those who would later take exception to publicist concepts of orders and jurisdiction such as those Augustinus had, one Conciliarist presented a theory on the status of the Pope-elect which is noteworthy. Joannes Gerson (1363-1429) criticized the view that one who was not a priest or bishop could become Pope and have the papal *plenitudo potestatis.* Behind this criticism was his opinion that this plenary power involved both orders and jurisdiction, and that one could not become the *Summus Pontifex* unless he were ordained. While he admitted that some jurisdiction would come to the *non sacerdos* elected Pope, Joannes ridiculed those who would equate the *plenitudo potestatis* with this jurisdiction. The absurd conclusion which would follow from such an opinion, he noted, was that a layman, even a woman, could be Pope and have this *plenitudo potestatis.*[23]

[21] *Summa de potestate ecclesiastica,* Q. LXXIV, 3, fol. 326.

[22] "Dicendum quod laico non committitur potestas spiritualis ut importat potestatem ordinis quod respicit corpus christi verum. Sed solum potestas jurisdictionis quod respicit corpus christi mysticum, unde talis potestas potest convenire clericis et laicis sicut in tali corpore simul conveniunt clerici et laici."—*loc. cit.*

[23] "Licet aliquis possit eligi in Papam non Sacerdos . . . ipse nihilominus non potest aut debet Summus Pontifex, nisi fuerit in Sacerdotem et Episcopum consecratus. Et quamvis ex electione possit aliquid Jurisdictionis habere; non tamen habet ante Consecrationem in Episcopum plenitudinem Ecclesiasticae potestatis tam Ordinis quam Jurisdictionis utriusque. . . . Hic autem consurgit aequivocatio non modica, propter Dominos Juristas, qui loquentes de plenitudine potestatis Papalis, solum loqui videntur de potestate Jurisdictionis, ex qua locutione videtur haec absurditas sequi, quod pure laicus, imo et femina posset esse Papa, et habere plenitudinem Ecclesiastice po-

An examination of the publicist literature also reveals that an important modification of the Decretist principle of *papa cum eligitur confirmatur* had been made by the fourteenth century. One of the arguments brought forth by the Colonna faction to prove that Pope Celestine's resignation was invalid was based on the premise that an ecclesiastical dignity, once obtained through legitimate confirmation, could be taken away only by a superior authority. The Pope, they argued, could not resign, since he had no superior but God alone.[24] In their reply to this charge, the publicists noted that the Pope's election was not confirmed by a higher superior, but by his consent to his own election. They then strengthened their position against the Colonna by reasoning that if one could become Pope by consent alone, he could also cease to be Pope by a similar act of his will.

> Cum ergo in talibus per eadem contrario modo facta res construatur et destruatur, sicut per consensum eligentium et assensum electi, quis praefectus est in Papam; sic per eadem contrario modo se habentia desinet esse Papa . . . Sed Papa, quia nullum habet superiorem quantum ad confirmationem visibilem, quae fit humano opere confirmatur per seipsum, ita quod suus assensus est confirmatio.[25]

testatis . . . possumus . . . dicere, quod plenitudo potestatis Ecclesiasticae, est potestas Ordinis et Jurisdictionis . . ."—*De potestate ecclesiastica*, in *Opera omnia* (ed. M. DuPin, 5 vols., Antwerpiae, 1706), II, 239. For the medieval development of the concept of *plenitudo potestatis*, see Tierney, *Conciliar Theory*, pp. 149-161 et passim.

[24] "Item ex eo quod nulla dignitas ecclesiastica post legitimam confirmationem potest tolli nisi per eius superiorem, sed papa solus est Deus maior, ergo a solo Deo tolli posse videtur."—Manifesto of May 10, 1297, as given in *Archiv für Literatur-und Kirchengeschichte*, V, 511; cf. Boase, *op. cit.*, p. 171.

[25] Giles of Rome, *De renuntiatione papae*, Cap. XVI, 2 (Rocaberti, II, 43); also John of Paris: "planum est quod hic intelligitur de dignitate que confirmatur per superiorem; sed assensus pape sine superiore confirmatio est, et ideo dissensus eius sine superiore cessio est."—*De potestate regia et papali*, Cap. XXV, ad 10 (ed. J. Leclercq, Paris: Librairie Philosophique J. Urin, 1942), p. 260; Augustinus

The publicists were here making very practical use of their canonical sources. The Decretists of the twelfth century had not discussed the need of the Pope's consent to his election when they formulated the expression *papa cum eligitur confirmatur.* By the mid-thirteenth century, however, the assent of the *electus* to his own election was recognized by the Decretalists as an essential part of the electoral process. The principle was soon applied to papal elections. Hostiensis, commenting on the election decree of Pope Nicholas II, declared:

> Illud quod ibi dicit, electus tamen sicut verus papa etc., intelligi debet de illo, qui jam consensit electioni, sive nominationi de se factae, cui ad potestatis plenitudinem consecratio nihil addit, ut ibi dicit. Ante consensum vero suum non potest dici, quod illam habeat potestatem, et proprie loquendo non potest dici electus; sed potius nominatur. . . .[26]

With this development by the Decretalists of the doctrine that the Pope-elect received his jurisdictional powers from the moment he accepted his election, the canonical foundations for our present discipline regarding the Pope-elect's authority, Canon 219, were completed.

SECTION 3. THE TEACHING OF JOANNES ANDREAE AND THE LATER CANONISTS

The canonistic writings which appeared after the Colonna

Triumphus: "sicut consentire electione de se facte est eius confirmatio, quia statim habet omnem papalem jurisdictionem, ita renunciare et dissentire eius jurisdictioni est eius depositio."—*Summa de potestate ecclesiastica,* Q. IV, 5, fol. 52.

[26] *Commentaria,* at X, I, 6, c. 6, s.v. *et receptus.* To illustrate the development of this teaching on the necessity of assent to one's election, note that twenty years previously Hostiensis had only commented: "Ex quo summus pontifex a duobus partibus electus est, voce electi computata ab omnibus recipiendus est, eligendo enim confirmatur et confirmando eligitur."—*Summa aurea, de electione et electi potestate,* n. 18; see also n. 25, where his general teaching on the question of *assensus* is given. The appearance of the clause "*dummodo electioni de se factae consentiat*" at X, I, 6, c. 33, stimulated Decretalist discussion of the effects of post-electoral consent.

manifestoes of 1297 indicate that the question of the layman elected Pope, raised only incidentally by the pro-papal publicists, was not to have a place in the discussions of the academic canonists. The attacks of the Colonna did of course have repercussions on canonical literature. Pope Boniface himself incorporated in the *Liber Sextus* a solemn proclamation of the Pope's right to resign.[27]

In their commentary on this decree, however, the canonists did not follow the line of argumentation taken by the publicists, and did not attempt to answer the Colonna point by point. Joannes Andreae did answer the objection made by the Colonna that the Pope could not resign because he had no higher superior. He argued that the precise reason why the Pope could abdicate was that he had no superior to look to for permission to resign.[28] However, Joannes did not make use of any of the arguments involving the distinction between orders and jurisdiction; therefore the occasion to go beyond the question of renunciation and to comment on the status of a layman elected Pope did not present itself to him as it had to the publicists.

The writer has examined a number of works of the fourteenth and fifteenth century canonists, none of which reveal any explicit mention of the problem of a lay Pope-elect's authority. The author of one of the many bulky repertories of Canon Law that appeared in the seventeenth and eighteenth centuries, Augustinus Barbosa, mentions in passing the opinion of Antonius de Rosellis (†1466) that the layman elected Pope would possess the power of jurisdiction.[29]

[27] VI°, I, 7, c. 1.

[28] "Inferiores praelati a suis praelatis confirmantur et instituuntur: unde non est mirum si sine ipsorum licentia renunciare non possunt: Sed Papa a nemine confirmatur: unde sicut sine superiore instituitur: ita sine superiore renunciet..."—*Glossa ordinaria,* on VI°, I, 7, c. 1, s.v. *videbantur.*

[29] *Collectanea doctorum tam veterum quam recentiorum in jus pontificium universum* (6 vols., Lugduni, 1656), V, 164. The massive work of Ferraris, *Prompta bibliotheca canonica, juridica, moralis, theologica...* (8 vols., Romae, 1885-1892) has nothing on the status of the layman elected Pope.

But this isolated reference seems to reflect the influence of publicist literature rather than of a canonical tradition. It is reasonably safe to assume that the remarks of Augustinus Triumphus on the layman elected Pope remained outside the main stream of canonistic thought.[30]

One might expect the later canonists to have appropriated for purposes of their own the interesting view of Augustinus Triumphus on the layman elected Pope, especially since it was but a logical conclusion of the theories of the Decretists on the jurisdictional authority possessed by the *papa electus non consecratus*. Several reasons suggest themselves as to why the canonists did not comment on this opinion of Augustinus. The storm of controversy over the power of the Pope to resign eventually died down. And the canonical sources were so filled with denials of the layman's power to take part in the government of the Church that the canonists perhaps preferred not to comment on the possibility of a layman possessing ordinary jurisdiction over the entire Church. The most likely solution, however, lies in the very structure of the later canonistic writings. The canonists of the Late Middle Ages were all too often content to fill their works with the *dicta* of the more revered canonists who wrote before them. There was little originality of thought, and the opinions of writers who were not canonists in the classical sense were generally considered as nonexistent.

ARTICLE 2. THE DECRETALS AND THE AUTHORITY OF RELIGIOUS SUPERIORESSES

A second area in which the medieval canonists might be

[30] Speaking of the defenders of Pope Boniface in the dispute with the Colonna, Ullmann writes: "If a layman were to be made Pope, these canonists said, he would assume the papal office immediately after giving his consent to the election."—"Medieval Views on Papal Abdication," *Irish Ecclesiastical Record,* LXXI (1949), 131. Since no reference to any individual canonist is given here, the writer presumes that Dr. Ullmann is using the word "canonist" in a more general sense to refer to the publicists, as the context seems to indicate.

expected to admit the ability of a particular class of laymen to possess jurisdiction is that involving the authority of religious superioresses. The Decretalists treated of the powers of women religious in their commentary on two important letters found in the Decretals of Gregory IX. The purpose of this article is to examine and analyze briefly the comments of Bernard of Parma, Innocent IV, and Hostiensis on these decretals. Their views provide an adequate cross section of thirteenth century canonical speculation on the nature of the authority the abbess had over her subjects.

The first of the letters which prompted the Decretalists to comment on the authority of religious superioresses is a letter of Pope Honorius addressed in the year 1222 to the abbot of the monastery of St. Michael in the diocese of Halberstadt. Pope Honorius informed the abbot of his receipt of a petition from the abbess of a monastery at Quedlinberg, evidently under the supervision of the abbot. It seems that the abbess had suspended from their offices and benefices a group of clerics and canonesses subject to her authority (*suae jurisdictioni subjecti*), and that they in turn had ignored her suspension on the grounds that abbesses had no authority to excommunicate. Since the disobedience of her subjects had not been corrected, the abbess referred the matter to the Pope. He answered by directing the abbot of St. Michael to compel the clerics and canonesses, under threat of censure, to observe the commands of the abbess, and to give her the reverence and obedience that was her due.[81]

[81] "Dilecta in Christo filia abbatissa de Bubrigen. transmissa nobis petitione monstravit, quod, quum ipsa plerumque canonicas suas et clericos suae jurisdictioni subjectos propter inobedientias et culpas eorum officio beneficioque suspendat iidem confisi ex eo, quod eadem abbatissa excommunicare eos non potest, suspensionem huiusmodi non observant, propter quod ipsorum excessus remanent incorrecti. Quocirca *discretioni tuae* mandamus, quatenus dictas canonicas et clericos, ut abbatissae praefatae obedientiam et reverentiam debitam impendentes, eius salubria monita et mandata observent, *monitione praemissa* ecclesiastica censura appellatione remota compellas." —X, I,

The other letter appears in the fifth book of the Decretals. It was one which had been sent by Pope Innocent III in 1210 to the bishops of Burgos and Palencia in Spain. Reports had reached Rome that certain abbesses of the region were preaching publicly, blessing their subjects, and even attempting to hear confessions. Pope Innocent condemned these practices as absurd; and noted that, although the Blessed Virgin was greater in dignity than all the Apostles, it was only to the Apostles that Christ had given the *claves regni coelorum.*[32]

Of the several areas of ecclesiastical authority touched by the two Popes in these decretals, the reference of Pope Honorius to the *jurisdictio* of the abbess over the clerics who administered the Sacraments to her subjects is most important for our purposes. The Decretalists interpreted the expression *"clerici suae jurisdictioni"* in a variety of ways. Bernard of Parma commented that this jurisdiction

33, c. 12; Potthast, n. 6857. Italicized words are the *partes decisae* as given by Friedberg. Hostiensis offered this explanation of the canonesses mentioned in the decretal: "Loquitur hae litera secundum consuetudinem theutonicorum. Sunt enim ibi in quibusdam ecclesiis quaedam canonicae saeculares, quae nec professionem faciunt, nec renunciant propriis, nec in communio vivunt. Habitum tamen quasi religiosum assumunt et habent singulae singulas cameras, et de praebendis et patrimoniis suis vivunt. In ecclesiis tamen ad horas canonicas conveniunt simul, et quando volunt nubunt..."—*Commentaria,* at X, I, 33, c. 12, s.v. *canonicas suas.* A similar explanation had earlier been given by Bernard of Parma in the *Glossa ordinaria* on this decretal.

[32] "Nova quaedam *nuper, de quibus miramur non modicum,* nostris sunt auribus intimata, quod abbatissae *videlicet, in Burgensi et in Palentinensi diocesibus constitutae,* moniales proprias benedicunt, ipsarum quoque confessiones in criminibus audiunt, et legentes evangelium praesumunt publice praedicare. Quum igitur id absonum sit pariter et absurdum,... mandamus, quatenus, ne id de cetero fiat, auctoritate curetis apostolica firmiter inhibere, quia, licet beatissima virgo Maria dignior et excellentior fuerit Apostolis universis, non tamen illi, sed istis Dominus claves regni coelorum commisit."—X, V, 38, c. 10; Potthast, n. 4143.

was not the full jurisdiction which only men could possess.[33] More interesting, however, is the opinion of Innocent IV. While he did not comment directly on the use of the word *jurisdictio* in regard to religious superioresses, he did give his own reason why abbesses could suspend clerics from office and benefice. By reason of custom, he said, these women possessed ordinary jurisdiction over their subjects.

> Nota hic, quod abbatissa potest suspendere clericos suos ab officio, et beneficio. Et hoc est ea ratione, quia ex consuetudine jurisdictionem habet ordinariam... alias enim est contra jus commune.[34]

For Hostiensis, this *jurisdictio* of the abbess was clearly an exception to the general rule regarding the possession of authority by women. His view seems to have been that these superioresses possessed every facet of jurisdiction except that involving the power of the keys.[35]

Before presenting the teaching of the Decretalists on women religious and the power of the keys, it should be noted that these canonists understood clearly that women were excluded from the possession of the power of orders. Gratian did make reference to the early ceremony known as the ordination of deaconesses.[36] The Decretalists also

[33] "Sic ergo mulier habet jurisdictionem.... Sed contra videtur quod mulier judicare non potest.... Dicas quod abbatissa habet jurisdictionem talem qualem, non ita plenam sicut vir habet."—*Glossa ordinaria*, on X, I, 33, c. 12, s.v. *jurisdictioni.*

[34] *Commentaria*, at X, I, 33, c. 12, s.v. *suspendant.* The distinction between ordinary and delegated power was clear by the time Innocent wrote. Cf. X, I, 31, c. 12.

[35] "Ergo mulier habet jurisdictionem.... Sed contra: quia mulier judicare non potest.... Sol. quod dicunt contaria regulariter obtinet. Fallit in mulieribus nobilibus, sicut reginis, comitissis et aliis similibus habentibus.... Fallit hoc et in muliere praelata eadem rationem ... talis tamen non habet plenam spiritualem jurisdictionem quia nec potest confessiones audire vel absolvere, nec alia, quae ad claves ecclesiae pertinent, exercere, quantumcunque, magna et nobilis habeatur..."—*Commentaria*, at X, I, 33, c. 12, s.v. *suae jurisdictioni.*

[36] "Diaconissa, que post ordinationem nubit, anathema sit."—C. XXVII, q. 1, c. 23 (rubric); see Sempere, "La mujer y la potestad de orden," *Revista Espanola de Derecho Canonico*, IX (1954), 845-

spoke of a certain *ordo* being received by abbesses when they were blessed, or of the exercise of this same quasi-order in connection with their choir functions. But they were also careful to point out that this was not an ecclesiastical order in the strict sense of the word.[37]

By the thirteenth century the sacerdotal *potestas clavium* was recognized as a power much wider in scope than the power to forgive sins. Excommunication was considered an act of jurisdiction involving the *potestas clavium*, which could not be possessed by laymen.[38]

The letter of Pope Innocent under study made it clear that women could in no way obtain this power of the keys. But while the decretal of Pope Honorius recognized the abbot of St. Michael as the one competent to excommunicate the subjects of the abbess should this be necessary, it left unanswered the question of the validity of the original suspension *ab officio* and *a beneficio* which the abbess had imposed upon her subjects. Bernard of Parma and Innocent

848 for the development of the canonists' views on the inability of women to possess orders.

[37] Innocent IV: "Moniales autem literatae dicunt officia; quia et ipsae possunt dici accipere aliquem ordinem in benedictione, unde etiam aliquae inter eas sunt diaconissae . . . qui ordo licet sufficiat ad officia dicenda, non tamen de septem ordinibus ecclesiae"—*Commentaria*, at X, III, 41, c. 1, s.v. *a scholaribus*. Hostiensis repeated Innocent's opinion in his *Commentaria* at the same decretal. The canonists frequently identified the abbess with the deaconess of the early church. E.g., Rufinus: "Hodie tamen huiusmodi diaconissae in ecclesia non inveniuntur, sed forte loco earum abbatisse ordinantur." —*Summa*, at C. XXVII, q. 1, c. 23; Bernard of Parma: "In matutinis forte poterant legere Evangelium, unde etiam diaconissae appellantur."—*Glossa ordinaria*, at X, V, 38, c. 10, s.v. *Evangelium*.

[38] Joannes Teutonicus noted that one suspended *ab officio* only, and not *a jurisdictione*, could himself excommunicate, "quia hoc jurisdictionis est."—*Glossa ordinaria*, on C. XXIV, q. 1, c. 4, s.v. *quia*. Regarding the requirement at X, V, 39, c. 50 that the heads of the military orders must be at least priests in order to absolve from excommunication, Hostiensis remarked: "si non esset sacerdos, non interdim hoc committere, quia nec istud posset, cum claves non habet." —*Commentaria*, at X, V, 39, c. 50, s.v. *presbiter esse debet*. See Tierney, *Conciliar Theory*, pp. 30-33, and the authors there cited.

IV seemed to have taken it for granted that the abbess in question had the authority to suspend her subjects from both their offices and their benefices.[39] Hostiensis, however, did not agree with this view. He believed the suspension invoked by the abbess had no juridic force. Suspension *ab officio,* he argued, was so connected with the power to excommunicate that it was in some way a part of the power of the keys. The abbess could only issue warnings and precepts to her subjects; she could not coerce them.[40] She could, however, withhold the prebends of a benefice from her subjects.[41]

The later canonists generally presented both sides of this debate, but favored the opinion of Hostiensis that denied the abbess power to suspend *ab officio.*[42]

[39] "Dicas ergo, quod potest suspendere ab officio et beneficio monachas suas, et clericos suae jurisdictioni subjectos, secundum quod hic satis innuitur, si inobedientes fuerint: habet enim administrationem temporalium et spiritualium . . ."—*Glossa ordinaria,* on X, I, 33, c. 12, s.v. *jurisdictioni.* Innocent IV's comment is given above p. 84.

[40] "Nihil dicit de sententia suspensionis, numquid ergo ipsam tenentur servare? sic secundum quosdam, quia ipsa suspendit . . . Respon. Verum est de facto. sed in alio loco istius literae non dicit quod jure hoc facere possit, non autem quod fit, sed quod fieri debeat. . . . Et ideo quicquid dicant alii, tu dicas, quod ad minus ab officio suspendere non potest: quia hoc quasi clavium est. et nomine censurae ecclesiasticae continentur, quod quia ipsam abbatissa exercere non potest, judicibus ad quos recurrat committitur. . . . Cum enim excommunicare, suspendere, et interdicere defectus jurisdictionis denegatur unum, et reliquum est denegandum."—*Commentaria,* at X, I, 33, c. 12, s.v. *observent.* "Ab abbatissam pertinent monitio, mandatum, sed non coerctio . . ."—*Commentaria* at the same decretal, s.v. *compellas.*

[41] ". . . nec suspendere, licet de facto posset prebendas suas subtrahere, quamvis alii dicant, quod suspendere potest."—*Commentaria,* at X, I, 33, c. 12.

[42] Aegidius de Bellamera's treatment of the subject is typical: "Queritur hic utrum abbatissa seu alia prelatissa ecclesiastica clericos sibi subditos . . . possit suspendere? dicunt quidem quod sic, quia ita fecit. . . . Sed secundum Hosti. illud fuit de facto unde nec hic dicitur quoad teneat suspensio. . . . Dico tamen, quod a beneficio posset suspendere; quia suspensio a beneficio non procedit a clave; nec comprehenditur sub censura: sed suspensio ab officio tantum. . . . Abba-

There was one exceptional circumstance in which the canonists believed that laymen could absolve from excommunication. This was the case in which one under censure was in danger of death, and no priest could be had to remove the excommunication. That confession of a non-sacramental or quasi-sacramental nature could be made to laymen when a person was in danger of death and no priest was available was a common teaching among medieval canonists and theologians alike. This led to the development of the view that under the same emergency conditions a layman could also absolve from excommunication. The opinion appeared explicitly in the writings of a number of thirteenth-century canonists.[43]

It is interesting to compare the views of the Decretalists regarding the possession of the power of the keys by women with the teaching of the contemporary theologians, who used a slightly different terminology. St. Thomas Aquinas, answering the objection that abbesses seemed to have spiritual power over their subjects, asserted that women had neither the *clavis ordinis* nor the *clavis jurisdictionis*. At the same time, however, he admitted that religious superioresses had a certain *usus clavium* in regard to the correction of their subjects, because of the dangers which would

tissa vero clavem non habet..."—*In decretales libros praelectiones*, at X, I, 33, c. 12.

[43] St. Raymond of Peñafort: "Item, nota, quod in articulo mortis potest absolvi excommunicatus, quacumque excommunicatione teneatur, a simplici sacerdote... immo etiam volunt plerique dicere, quod a laico..."—*Summa*, III, *de inquisitionibus et purgationibus*, n. 58; Hostiensis: "In quo casue de qualibet excommunicatione, et a quolibet etiam laico quilibet absolvi potest."—*Commentaria*, at X, I, 31, c. 11. For the origin and history of the medieval practice of confession to laymen, see Teetaert, *La confession aux laïques dans l'Eglise latine depuis le VIIe jusque' au XIVe siecle*, Universitas Catholica Lovaniensis Dissertationes ad gradum magistri in Facultate Theologica consequendum conscriptae; Series II, n. 17 (Paris: J. Gebalda, 1926), which contains extensive quotations from the canonists; also the shorter summary of the theological debate regarding the practice, given by Doronzo, *Tractatus dogmaticus de poenitentia* (4 vols., Milwaukiae: Ex typographia Bruce, 1949-1953), IV, 662-723.

be present were men to live in the monasteries of women.[44]

In the letter of Pope Innocent III to the bishops of Burgos and Palencia, women religious were strictly forbidden to preach publicly. Commenting on this prohibition, the Decretalists frequently cited a canon in the *Decretum* which forbade women to teach men when the faithful assembled.

> Mulier, quamvis docta et sancta, viros in conventu docere non praesumat. Laicus autem praesentibus clericis (nisi ipsis rogantibus) docere non audeat.[45]

The presence of the phrase "nisi ipsis rogantibus" in this canon contributed to the rapid development of the common opinion of the thirteenth century canonists that any layman could be delegated to preach, at least by special privilege of the Pope.[46] Together with Innocent's implied distinction

[44] "Dicendum quod mulier, secundum apostolum, est in statu subjectionis; et ideo ipsa non potest habere aliquam jurisdictionem spiritualem... unde mulier non habet neque clavem ordinis, nec clavem jurisdictionis. Sed mulieri committitur aliquis usus clavium, sicut habere correptionem in subditas mulieres, propter periculum quod imminere possit, si viri mulieribus cohabitarent."—*Comment. in IV*, Dist. XIX, Q. 1, a. 1, q. 3; *Opera omnia*, X, 547.

[45] D. XXIII, c. 29, which contains c. 99 and 98 of the *Statuta Ecclesiae Antiqua* as found in Bruns, I, 150. The early Decretists noted at this canon that women religious superiors could teach their subjects. Thus the *Summa Parisiensis*: "De muliere dixerat quod non debet offerre incensum circa altare... et ea occasione aliud removendum removet, ne scilicet doceat viros, nam mulieres potest abbatissa..."—At D. XXIII, c. 29, s.v. *mulier*.

[46] Thus Joannes Teutonicus: "Sed nunquid auctoritate episcopi potest laicus aliquid constituere in ecclesia? videtur, quod praedicare potest invitatus a clericis 23 distinctio mulier [c. 29]. Dic cum H[uguccio] quod non potest ex delegatione episcopi causas spirituales tractare, nec excommunicare.... Et quod dicitur de praedicatione speciale est..."—*Glossa ordinaria*, on D. XCVI, c. 1, s.v. *praeter Romanum Pontificem;* also: "...laici praedicant, et mulieres de licentia sacerdotis..."—*Glossa ordinaria*, on C. XVI, q. 1, c. 19, s.v. *praeter sacerdotes*. Panormitanus qualified his general agreement with this gloss with the remark: "Sed inquantum illa glossa dicit de muliere, non puto glossam verum dicere; quia est virile officium..."—*Commentaria*, at X, II, 1, 2. Joannes explained preaching by lay members of the military orders in this way: "Sed illi non dicuntur laici, cum sint Deo devoti... vel ipsi habent hoc ex speciali privilegio."—*Glossa*

between private and public preaching, this teaching provided the background for the common Decretalist opinion that abbesses, while forbidden to preach in public, could in their own cloister instruct their subjects, and preach to them as well.[47]

In view of this speculation by the Decretalists on the authority possessed by religious superioresses, the question can be raised as to whether or not these canonists actually meant to attribute to abbesses any share of what we now understand to be ecclesiastical jurisdiction, namely, the public power which the Church possesses to rule the faithful.[48]

The canonists after the Council of Trent engaged in frequent debate on the possibility of women being delegated the power of jurisdiction, and on the further question as to whether or not the Church had ever given women such authority. Their lengthy discussions usually centered around

ordinaria, on D. XXIII, c. 29, s.v. *laicus.* In his *Rosarium,* Guido de Baysio commented on this gloss: "Adde idem Hug[uccio] no. hic, scilicet quod habent a Papa liberam licentiam docendi et praedicandi populo. secundum La[urentius]."

[47] "In matutinis forte poterant legere Evangelium, unde etiam diaconissae appellantur."—*Glossa ordinaria,* on X, V, 38, c. 10, s.v. *Evangelium;* Hostiensis: "... si privatim in capitulo solis monialibus suis regulam exponeret, vel ad instructionem morum aliqua exempla bona vel alia simplicia verba proponeret hoc non reprobaretur."—*Commentaria,* at X, V, 38, c. 10, s.v. *publica;* also Guido de Baysio: "In conventu publico, id est, ecclesia ascendendo pulpitum, et faciendo sermonem ad populum. Sed si est Abbatissa, secrete, in claustro vel capitulo vel choro docere potest suas Monachas, vel conversas, et etiam conversos, et eis praedicare."—*Rosarium,* at D. XXIII, c. 29. By the early part of the thirteenth century the canonists were teaching specifically that preaching was not an act which involved the power of orders. Joannes Teutonicus wrote regarding preaching by subdeacons: "... ita quia praelationem et curam animarum habere potest ... praedicat ergo ratione praelationis, sed non ratione ordinis." —*Glossa ordinaria,* on C. XVI, q. 1, c. 19, s.v. *sacerdotes.* Cf. X, I, 14, c. 5, where the practice of giving subdeacons charge of a parochial church is recognized.

[48] "Potestas publica regendi fideles ad finem suum supernaturalem ..."—Vermeersch-Creusen, *Epitome juris canonici,* I, 214.

the two decretals presented in this article, and the opinions of the medieval canonists who commented on them.[49]

The fundamental difficulty, it seems, lies in the understanding of the word *jurisdictio* as used by Pope Honorius in reference to abbesses.[50] One modern writer has noted that the word here could be taken to mean nothing more than administration, inasmuch as it had frequently been used with this connotation prior to the time Honorius wrote (1220).

> It is known with certainty that from 1215 jurisdiction was understood to be the public power of ruling a perfect society, embracing accordingly a legislative, a judicial and a coercive power. However, it cannot be presumed that from that date forward the word "jurisdiction," no matter where it appeared, was always employed in that meaning. It could still have been employed, as it had been employed in the past, to signify administration.[51]

This is certainly a possibility, so much so, in fact, that it would seem imprudent to hold that Pope Honorius was definitely using *jurisdictio* with its present meaning.

From this it does not follow, however, that the Decretalists who repeated this statement of Honorius regarding the abbess' *jurisdictio* were also using the word only to connote administration. The writer's opinion is that Innocent IV's remark giving the abbess ordinary jurisdiction by reason of custom very probably involved more than mere administration of the monastery's temporal goods. Innocent's *Commentaria* was written around the year 1251. Sometime between 1215 and 1250, if Van de Kerckhove's conclusions are correct, *jurisdictio* became the common word used by the canonists to express the public power of the

[49] A summary of the opinions of the canonists after Trent on these questions is given by Bowe, *Religious Superioresses*, The Catholic University of America Canon Law Studies, n. 228 (Washington, D.C.: The Catholic University of America Press, 1946), pp. 25-31.

[50] X, I, 33, c. 12; above, p. 144?.

[51] Bowe, *op. cit.*, pp. 23-24.

Church to rule and govern.[52] This being the case, the presumption should lie in favor of Innocent's using the word in the broader sense of *potestas regiminis.*

On the other hand, Hostiensis was more cautious in his approach to the problem. He did not so much as mention Innocent's opinion regarding the possession of ordinary jurisdiction by women religious. Perhaps the reason for this was that he wrote at a much later date, and was more aware of the implications of such a statement. He was firm in denying abbesses any authority involving the *potestas clavium;* but whether or not it was his custom to consider every act of ecclesiastical jurisdiction an exercise of the power of the keys is not known.

A variety of interpretations, then, can be given to the Decretalists' opinions regarding the authority of the abbess. The whole matter offers possibilities for a great deal of future research. The canonical opinions presented in this brief summary of Decretalist theorizing on two small decretals, however, indicate that the medieval canonists were willing to admit of exceptions to their general principle that only the clergy could possess jurisdictional authority in the Church.

[52] See above, p. 17.

CONCLUSIONS

1. Because the medieval canonists only gradually developed clear concepts of the distinction between the powers of orders and of jurisdiction, it is difficult to determine in every case the kind and degree of authority individual canonists had in mind when discussing the layman and the Church's governmental powers. (pp. 15-18)

2. The description of the two classes of Christians given by Gratian at C. XII, q. 1, c. 7 provided the medieval canonists with their basic definitions of the clerical and lay states. The lay state was here described only in a negative way, by contrasting the layman's activities with those of the faithful who were called to a life of perfection, the clerics and religious. (pp. 20-26)

3. This fundamental canon, with its opening words *Duo sunt genera Christianorum,* was of particular importance in that it gave the canonists a legal basis in the *Decretum* to support a strict juridic dichotomy between clergy and laity, and between their respective rights and obligations. It was frequently cited in defense of the Church's rights against the encroachments of laymen. (pp. 24-25)

4. At times the word *clericus* was used by the canonists in a wide sense to include religious. Regularly, however, its meaning was restricted to those who had entered the clerical state by the reception of first tonsure. (pp. 26-30)

5. The variety of enumerations of the ecclesiastical orders appearing in the *Decretum* led the early canonists to speculate on the nature of the ancient order of *psalmistatus.* (pp. 33-34)

The twelfth century Decretists in general did not consider this to be an order existing in their day. However, by the time of Joannes Teutonicus the canonists had clearly identified the *psalmistatus* as an order, and had equated it with first tonsure. The declaration of Pope Innocent III that the *ordo clericatus* was conferred by monastic tonsure was largely responsible for this teaching. (pp. 34-38)

6. Necessary though it was, the attack of the canonists upon the variety of abuses connected with the proprietary church system can be held responsible, in large measure, for the creation of the negative atmosphere which was to surround all medieval canonistic theory regarding the layman's place in the life of the Church. (pp. 43-55)

7. By their speculation on the nature of the *jus praesentandi* mentioned in the *Decretum*, the Decretists of the twelfth century laid the canonical foundations for our present law on the right of patronage. (pp. 47-54)

8. Pope Alexander III's extensive application of these Decretist principles to practical cases resulted in the growth of the *jus patronatus* into a well developed canonical institute by 1180. (pp. 54-55)

9. The negative attitude of the medieval canonists toward the layman is characterized by the appearance of a variety of stereotyped expressions in their writings, their general principle being that laymen have no authority in ecclesiastical matters. This negative attitude, while unfortunate, is understandable, particularly in view of the fact that many of the lay abuses prevalent when Gratian wrote remained as serious problems for the Church throughout the High Middle Ages. (pp. 56-65)

10. The development of a number of canonistic theories on the corporate structure of the Church during the twelfth and thirteenth centuries had little or no effect upon Decretalist teaching regarding the juridic status of laymen. (pp-65-66)

11. The status of the layman elected Pope was not discussed by the Decretists of the twelfth century. Out of their comments on the election decree of Pope Nicholas II, however, there did develop the doctrine that the Pope-elect not a bishop would possess the power of jurisdiction over the

Church from the moment of his election. Implied in this is the teaching that a layman elected Pope would have a similar authority. (pp. 68-73).

12. That a layman elected Pope would have the power of jurisdiction from the moment of his assent to his election became explicit in the pro-papal publicist literature of the fourteenth century. Augustinus Triumphus was very likely the first to express this view; however, his teaching made little impression on the canonists who wrote after him. (pp. 73-81)

13. The Decretalists seem to have attributed to religious superioresses some share of ecclesiastical jurisdiction as we know it today. However, there is need of additional studies on the terminology of the canonists in regard to jurisdiction and the *potestas clavium* before the question can be resolved with certainty. (pp. 81-91)

BIBLIOGRAPHY

SOURCES

MEDIEVAL CANONISTS

Aegidius de Bellamera, *In decretales libros praelectiones*, 6 vols., Lugduni, 1548-1549.

Alexander III, see Rolandus Bandinelli.

Bernardus Parmensis, *Glossa ordinaria* to the Decretals, in *Decretales D. Gregorii Papae IX ... una cum glossis ...* Romae, 1582.

Durandus, see Guilielmus Durantis.

Guido de Baysio (Archidiaconus), *In Sextum Decretalium commentaria*, Venetiis, 1577.

———, *Rosarium seu in Decretorum volumen commentaria*, Venetiis, 1577.

Guilielmus Durantis, *Rationale divinorum officiorum*, Venetiis, 1519.

———, *Speculum juris Guilielmi Durandi*, 4 vols., Venetiis, 1577.

Henricus de Bohic, *Henrici Boich ... in quinque decretalium libros commentaria*, Venetiis, 1576.

Hostiensis (Henricus de Segusio), *Commentaria in libros decretalium*, 6 vols., Venetiis, 1581.

———, *Summa aurea*, Venetiis, 1570.

Innocentius IV, *Commentaria in quinque libros decretalium*, Venetiis, 1570.

Joannes Andreae, *Glossa ordinaria* to the *Liber Sextus*, in *Liber Sextus Decretalium D. Bonifacii Papae VIII ...* Romae, 1582.

Joannes Teutonicus, *Glossa ordinaria* to the *Decretum*, in *Decretum Gratiani ... cum glossis*, Rome, 1592.

Panormitanus (Nicholas de Tudeschis), *Commentaria in quinque libros decretalium*, 5 vols. in 7, Venetiis, 1588.

Paucapalea, *Die Summa des Paucapalea über das Decretum Gratiani*, ed. J. F. v. Schulte, Giessen: Verlag von Emil Roth, 1890.

Raymundus de Pennaforte, St., *Summa Sti. Raymundi de Peniafort ... de poenitentia et matrimonio*, Romae, 1603.

Rolandus Bandinelli (Alexander III), *Die Summa Magistri Rolandi nachals Papstes Alexander III*, ed. F. Thaner, Innsbruck: Verlag der Wagner'schen Universitaets-Buchhandlung, 1874.

Rufinus, *Die Summa Decretorum des Magister Rufinus*, ed. H. Singer, Paderborn: Verlag von Ferdinand Schoningh, 1902.

Stephanus Tornacensis, *Die Summa des Stephanus Tornacensis über das Decretum Gratiani*, ed. J. F. v. Schulte, Giessen: Verlag von Emil Roth, 1891.

Summa Parisiensis, *The Summa Parisiensis on the Decretum Gratiani*, ed. T. P. McLaughlin, Toronto: The Pontifical Institute of Mediaeval Studies, 1952.

OTHER MEDIEVAL WRITERS

Augustinus Triumphus, *Summa de potestate ecclesiastica*, Augustae Vindelicorum, 1473.

———, *Tractatus brevis de duplici potestate praelatorum et laicorum*, in Scholz, *Die Publizistik zur Zeit Phillipps des Schönen und Bonifaz VIII* (Stuttgart, 1903), pp. 486-501.

Giles of Rome (Egidio Colonna), *De renuntiatione papae*, in *Bibliotheca maxima pontificia*, II, 1-64.

Joannes Gerson, *De potestate ecclesiastica*, in *Opera omnia* (ed. M. Du Pin, 5 vols., Antwerpiae, 1706), II, 226-258.

John of Paris, *De potestate regia et papali*, ed. J. Leclercq, Paris: Librairie Philosophique J. Urin, 1942.

Peter John Olivi, *De renuntiatione papae*, ed. P. L. Oliger, in *Archivum Franciscum Historicum*, XI (1918), 340-366.

Thomas Aquinas, Saint, *Opera omnia . . . eds.* S. Frette et Pauli Mare, 34 vols., Parisiis: L. Vives, 1871-1880.

COLLECTED WORKS

Acta Apostolicae Sedis, Commentarium Officiale, Romae, 1909; Civitate Vaticana, 1929—.

Ancient Christian Writers, eds. J. Quasten and J. Plumpe; Vol. I, *The Epistles of St. Clement of Rome and St. Ignatius of Antioch*, tr. by James Kleist, S.J., 1949; Westminster, Md.: The Newman Press.

Antiquae collectiones decretalium, ed. A. Augustinus, Ilerdae, 1576.

Archiv für Literatur-und Kirchengeschichte, eds. P. Denifle, F. Ehrle, Freiburg, 1895.

Archivum Franciscanum Historicum, Florence, 1908—.

Bibliotheca maxima pontificia, ed. J. Thomas de Rocaberti, 21 vols., Romae, 1697-1699.

Bruns, H. T., *Canones Apostolorum et Conciliorum saeculorum* IV-VII, 2 vols., Berolini: G. Remerius, 1839.

Codex Juris Canonici, Pii X Pontificis Maximi jussu digestus, Benedicti Papae XV auctoritate promulgatus, praefatione, fontium, annotatione et indice analytico-alphabetico ab Emo Petro Card. Gasparri auctus, Romae, Typis Polyglottis Vaticanis, 1917; reimpressio, 1934.

Corpus Juris Canonici, ed. Lipsiensis secunda, post Aemilii Richteri curas . . . instruxit Aemilius Friedberg, 2 vols., Lipsiae, 1879-1881.

Decretales D. Gregorii Papae IX, suae integritati una cum glossis restitutae, cum privilegio Gregorii XIII, Pont. Max... Romae, 1582.

Decretum Gratiani emendatum et notationibus illustratum cum glossis, Gregorii XIII, Pont. Max., jussu editum, 2 vols., Romae, 1592.

Enchiridion symbolorum definitionum et declarationum de rebus fidei et morum, eds. H. Denzinger, C. Bannwart, J. Umberg, 26. ed., Friburgi Brisgoviae: Herder & Co., 1946.

Jaffé, P., *Regesta Pontificum Romanorum ab condita Ecclesia ad annum post Christum natum MCXCVIII*, 2. ed. correctam et auctam auspiciis Guilielmi Wattenbach, curaverunt, S. Loewenfeld, F. Kaltenbrunner, P. Ewald, 2 vols., Lipsiae, 1885-1888.

Hinschius, P., *Decretales Pseudo-Isidorianae et Capitula Angilramni*, Lipsiae, 1863.

Liber Sextus Decretalium D. Bonifacii Papae VIII, suae integritati cum Clementinis et Extravagantibus, earumque glossis restitutis, Romae, 1582.

Mansi, Joannes, *Sacrorum Conciliorum nova et amplissima collectio*, 53 vols. in 60, Parisiis, Arnhem, Lipsiae, 1901.

Migne, J. P., *Patrologiae cursus completus, series latina*, 221 vols., Parisiis, 1844-1855.

Monumenta Germaniae Historica, 188 vols. incomplete, Hannoverae, 1826—; *Legum sectio IV*, I, ed. L. Weiland, 1893; *Epistolarum sectio II*, I, edd. P. Ewald and M. Hartman, 1887-1928.

Quinque compilationes antiquae nec non collectio canonum Lipsiensis, ed. Aemilius Friedberg (first published Leipzig, 1882), Graz: Akademische Druck-U. Verlagsanstalt, 1956.

Pontificale Romanum in tres partes distributum, 3 vols., Parisiis: J. Leroux et Jouby, 1852.

Potthast, A., *Regesta Pontificum Romanorum inde ab anno post Christum natum MCXCVIII ad annum MCCCIV*, 2 vols., Berolini, 1874-1875.

Scholz, R., *Die Publizistik zur Zeit Phillipps des Schönen und Bonifaz' VIII*, Stuttgart: Verlag von F. Enke, 1903.

Studia Gratiana post octava Decreti saecularia, Bononiae, 1953—.

Reference Works

A Greek-English Lexicon, eds. Henry G. Liddell, Robert Scott et. al., 9. ed., Oxford: Clarendon Press, 1942.

Anciaux, P., *La théologie du sacrament de pénitence au XIIe siècle*, Universitas Catholica Lovaniensis Dissertationes ad gradum magistri in Facultate Theologica vel in Facultate Juris Canonici consequendum conscriptae, Series II, n. 41, Louvain: E. Nauwelaerts, 1949.

Barbosa, Augustinus, *Collectanea doctorum tam veterum quam recentiorum in jus pontificium universum*, 6 vols., Lugduni, 1656.

Berardi, Carolus, *Gratiani canones genuini ab apocryphis discreti*, 3 vols., Venetiis, 1777.

Berger, Adolf, *Encyclopedic Dictionary of Roman Law*, Vol. XLIII, part 2, of the *Transactions of the American Philosophical Society*, Philadelphia, 1953.

Boase, T. S., *Boniface VIII*, London: Constable and Co., 1933.

Bowe, Thomas J., *Religious Superioresses*, The Catholic University of America Canon Law Studies, n. 228, Washington, D.C.: The Catholic University of America Press, 1946.

Brockhaus, Thomas A., *Religious who are known as Conversi*, The Catholic University of America Canon Law Studies, n. 225, Washington, D.C.: The Catholic University of America Press, 1945.

Cappello, Felix, *Tractatus canonico-moralis de Sacramentis*, 5 vols.; Vol. IV, 3. ed., 1951; Romae, Marietti.

Congar, Yves M. J., *Lay People in the Church, A Study for a Theology of the Laity*, trans. D. Attwater, Westminster, Md.: Newman Press, 1957.

Dictionnaire de droit canonique, eds. A. Villien, E. Magnin, A. Amanieu, R. Naz, Paris, 1924—.

Doronzo, Emmanuel, O.M.I., *Tractatus dogmaticus de poenitentia*, 4 vols., Milwaukiae: Ex Typographia Bruce, 1949-1953.

Downs, John, *The Concept of Clerical Immunity*, The Catholic University of America Canon Law Studies, n. 126, Washington, D.C.: The Catholic University of America Press, 1941.

Du Cange, Charles Du Fresne, *Glossarum mediae et infimae latinitatis*, ed. nova aucta . . . a Leopold Favre [1. ed. 1678-1736], 10 vols., Paris, 1937-1938.

Fagnanus, Prosperus, *Jus canonicum seu commentaria absolutissima in quinque decretalium libros*, 3 vols., Venetiis, 1729.

Falletti, L., "Guillaume Durand," *Dictionnaire de droit canonique*, V, 1014-1074.

Feine, H. E., *Kirchliche Rechtsgeschichte, I. Band: Die katholische Kirche*, Weimar: Herman Nachfolger, 1955.

Ferraris, L., *Prompta bibliotheca canonica, juridica, moralis, theologica*, 9 vols., ed. novissima, Romae, 1885-1899.

Fournier, P. et Le Bras, G., *Histoire des collections canoniques en occident*, 2 vols., Paris, 1931-1932.

Gasparri, P., *Tractatus canonicus de sacra ordinatione*, 2 vols., Paris: Delhomme et Briquet, 1893-1894.

Heintschel, Donald E., *The Mediaeval Concept of an Ecclesiastical Office*, The Catholic University of America Canon Law Studies,

n. 363, Washington, D.C.: The Catholic University of America Press, 1956.

Hughes, Philip, *A History of the Church,* 3 vols., New York: Sheed and Ward, 1947-1949.

Kantorowicz, *The King's Two Bodies, A Study in Mediaeval Political Theology,* Princeton, N.J.: Princeton University Press, 1957.

Kurtscheid, B., *Historia juris canonici, Historica institutorum ab Ecclesiae fundatione usque ad Gratianum,* Romae: Officium Libri Catholici, 1956.

Kuttner, Stephan, *Repertorium der Kanonistik, Prodromus corporis glossarum,* I, Studi et testi, 71, Citta del Vaticano, 1937.

Le Bras, Gabriel, "Canon Law," *The Legacy of the Middle Ages,* ed., C. Crump and E. Jacob, Oxford: Clarendon Press, 1951, pp. 321-361.

Lefebvre, Ch., "Panormitain," *Dictionnaire de droit canonique,* Fasc. XXXV (1957), 1195-1215.

March, Joaquin, *Derechos y Deberes de los Seglares en la Vida Social de la Iglesia,* Barcelona: Herder, 1954.

Marschesi, F., "De rationibus quae intercedunt inter Ecclesiam et res publicas in Gratiani Decreto," *Studia Gratiana post octava Decreti saecularia,* III (1955), 181-195.

McBride, Thomas, *Incardination and Excardination of Seculars,* The Catholic University of America Canon Law Studies, n. 145, Washington, D.C.: The Catholic University of America Press, 1941.

Philips, G., *The Role of the Laity in the Church,* trans. J. Gilbert and J. Moudry, Chicago: Fides Publishers, 1957.

Schulte, J. F. v., *Die Geschichte der Quellen und Literatur des canoischen Rects von Gratian bis auf die Gegenwart,* 3 vols., Stuttgart: Verlag von Ferdinand Enke, 1875-1880.

Sokolich, A., *Canonical Provisions for Universities and Colleges,* The Catholic University of America Canon Law Studies, n. 373, Washington, D.C.: The Catholic University of America Press, 1956.

Stickler, Alphonsus, *Historia juris canonici latini, I, Historia fontium,* Augustae Taurinorum, 1950.

Stutz, Ulrich, "The Proprietary Church as an Element of Mediaeval Germanic Ecclesiastical Law," in *Studies in Mediaeval History,* ed. G. Barraclough (2 vols., Oxford: Blackwell and Mott, 1938), II, 35-70.

Teetaert, P. Amedee, *La confession aux laïques dans l'Eglise latine depuis le VIIIe jusque' au XIVe siecle,* Universitas Catholica Lovaniensis Dissertationes ad gradum magistri in Facultate Theologica consequendum conscriptae; Series II, n. 17, Paris: J. Gebalda, 1926.

Thomas, P., *Le droit de propriété des laïques sur les églises et le patronage laïque au moyen âge*, Paris, 1906.

Tierney, Brian, *Foundations of the Conciliar Theory, The Contribution of the Medieval Canonists from Gratian to the Great Schism*, Cambridge Studies in Medieval Life and Thought, Vol. 4 (N.S.), Cambridge: Cambridge University Press, 1955.

Tirado, Victor, *De jurisdictionis acceptatione in jure ecclesiastico*, Romae: Collegium Internationale, 1940.

Tixeront, J., *Holy Orders and Ordination, A Study in the History of Dogma*, tr. by S. Raemers, St. Louis: Herder, 1928.

Ullmann, Walter, *Medieval Papalism, The Political Theories of the Medieval Canonists*, The Maitland Memorial Lectures Delivered in the University of Cambridge, Lent Term, 1948, London: Methuen and Co., 1949.

Van Hove, Alphonsus, *Prolegomena ad Codicem Juris Canonici*, 2. ed., Mechliniae: H. Dessain, 1945.

Vermeersch, A., and Creusen, J., *Epitome juris canonici*, 3 vols.; Vol. I, 7. ed., 1949; Mechliniae-Romae: H. Dessain.

Unpublished Work

Benson, Robert L., "From Election to Consecration: Studies on the Constitutional Status of an *Electus* in the High Middle Ages," unpublished Ph.D. dissertation, Princeton University, 1957.

Articles

Kuttner, Stephan, "Bernardus Compostellanus Antiquus," *Traditio*, I (1943), 277-340.

———, "Cardinalis: The History of a Canonical Concept," *Traditio*, III (1945), 129-214.

———, "The Father of the Science of Canan Law," *The Jurist*, I (1941), 2-19.

———, "The Scientific Investigation of Mediaeval Canon Law: The Need and the Opportunity," *Speculum*, XIV (1949), 493-501.

———, "Zur Entstehungsgeschichte der Summa de casibus des hl. Raymund von Penyafort," *Zeitschrift der Savigny Stiftung für Rechtsgeschichte, Kanonistische Abteilung*, XXXIX (1953), 419-434.

Kuttner, S., and Rathbone, E., "Anglo-Norman Canonists of the Twelfth Century," *Traditio*, VII (1949-1951), 279-339.

Kuttner, S., and Smalley, Beryl, "The *Glossa Ordinaria* to the Gregorian Decretals," *The English Historical Review*, LX (1945), 97-105.

Seckel, E., "Studien zu Benedictus Levita, VIII," *Zeitschrift der Savigny Stiftung für Rechtsgeschichte, Kanonistische Abteilung*, XXIV (1935), 1-112.

Sempere, G., "La mujer y la potestad de orden," *Revista Espanola de Derecho Canonico,* IX (1954), 841-869.

Sigur, Alexander, "Lay Cooperation with the Magisterium," *The Jurist,* XIII (1953), 268-297.

Stickler, A. M., "Concerning the Political Theories of the Medieval Canonists," review of Ullmann, W., *Medieval Papalism, Traditio,* VII (1949-1951), 450-463.

Stutz, Ulrich, "Gratian und die Eigenkirchen," *Zeitschrift der Savigny Stiftung für Rechtsgeschichte, Kanonistische Abteilung,* I (1911), 1-33.

Ullman, Walter, "Medieval Views on Papal Abdication," *Irish Ecclesiastical Record,* LXXI (1949), 125-133.

Van de Kerchhove, M., "De notione jurisdictionis apud Decretistas et priores Decretalists," *Jus Pontificium,* XVIII (1938), 10-14.

Wilks, M., "Papa est Nomen Jurisdictionis: Augustinus Triumphus and the Papal Vicariate of Christ," *The Journal of Theological Studies,* VIII (1957), 71-91; 256-271.

Periodicals

Apollinaris, Romae, 1928—.

English Historical Review, The, London, 1886—.

Irish Ecclesiastical Record, The, Fifth Series, Dublin, 1913—.

Journal of Theological Studies, The, New Series, Oxford, 1950—.

Jurist, The, Washington, D.C., 1941—.

Jus Pontificium, Romae, 1921—.

Revista Espanola de Derecho Canonico, Salamanca, 1946—.

Speculum, Cambridge, Mass., 1926—.

Traditio, New York, 1943—.

Zeitschrift der Savigny Stiftung für Rechtsgeschichte, Weimar, 1880—.

ALPHABETICAL INDEX

BIOGRAPHICAL NOTE

Ronald John Cox was born June 21, 1929, at Martins Ferry, Ohio, and there attended St. Mary's Parochial School. After graduation from Central Catholic High School in Wheeling, W. Va., he entered Xavier University in Cincinnati, Ohio, in September of 1947. In January of 1949 he enrolled in St. Gregory Seminary in that city, and that fall entered Mt. St. Mary Seminary of the West, Norwood, Ohio, to begin his philosophical and theological studies. In September of 1952 he was transferred to the Theological College of the Catholic University of America, where he obtained the degree of the Licentiate in Sacred Theology in May, 1955. He was ordained to the priesthood on May 28, 1955, in Martins Ferry, Ohio. In September of that year he enrolled in the School of Canon Law at the Catholic University of America. He received the degree of the Baccalaureate in Canon Law in June, 1956, and the degree of the Licentiate in Canon Law in June, 1957.

CANON LAW STUDIES*

392. Adams, Rev. Donald E., A.B., J.C.L., The truth required in the *preces* for rescripts.
393. Begin, Rev. Raymond F., A.B., S.T.L., J.C.L., Natural law and positive law.
394. Clancy, Rev. Walter B., A.B., J.C.L., The rites and ceremonies of sacred ordination.
395. Cox, Rev. Ronald J., S.T.L., J.C.L., A study of the juridic status of laymen in the writing of the medieval canonists.
396. Demers, Rev. Francis L., O.M.I., A.B., J.C.L., Temporal administration of the religious house in a non-exempt clerical pontifical institute.
397. Dziadosz, Rev. Henry J., M.A., S.T.L., J.C.L., The provisions of the Decree "Spiritus Sancti munera": the law for the extraordinary minister of confirmation.
398. Gerhardt, Rev. Bernard C., A.B., S.T.L., J.C.L., Interpretation of rescripts.
399. Hackett, Rev. John H., A.B., J.C.L., The concept of public order.
400. Murphy, Rev. Richard J., O.M.I., S.T.L., J.C.L., The canonico-juridical status of a communist.
401. O'Connor, Rev. David, M.S.SS.T., J.C.L., Parochial relations and co-operation of the religious and secular clergy.

* For a complete list of the available numbers of this series apply to the Catholic University of America Press, 620 Michigan Avenue, N.E., Washington (17), D.C., for a general catalogue.

www.ingramcontent.com/pod-product-compliance
Lightning Source LLC
LaVergne TN
LVHW050200080826
844660LV00012B/325

9780813225555